I Am Here But I Am Not

The Poetry of
Heidi Schneider
1986-2020

FIRST EDITION

Jason Schneider

ISBN: 978-1-66784-701-6 (hc)
ISBN: 978-1-66784-702-3 (ebook)

Design by Lisa Nicole Ewart

Printed in the United States of America

CONTENTS

I know her, yet not.
She is in my dreams
She is Angel Fairylike
with wings of gold
She cannot listen
to what she's been told
Yet questions it with ever love
    so gentle and so kind.
Yet she demands to know:
"Is this where God
    and Heaven lie ?"
Or is this the road
to trickery and lies?"
She lies back and cries
The eternal question
haunts her,
But she is comforted by
Guardian Angels from above.
Yet she knows one thing
    as she looks at me
    in steady glance,
    her eyes in ever blue,
"I am not from this world,"
    she says,
"I'd like to know, are you?"

HEIDI SCHNEIDER

INTRODUCTION

Heidi Schneider was a poetic prodigy. At age 11 she presented me with a draft of her first poem, scrawled in pencil on a scrap of paper. I was astounded by its transcendent quality, the felicity of its expression, and the majestic cadences and rhythms of its language. I instantly knew it was a work of genius, and, like all of Heidi's poetry, it is an authentic and compelling representation of her state of consciousness at the instant of its creation. Astonished by Heidi's dedication and passion for turning out a succession of poems of extraordinary power and insight, I finally asked her, "Why do you write poetry?" "Because I can't *not* write poetry," she replied. That, of course, is the very best answer there is.

Heidi's poetry encompasses the full range of her experiences and emotions, from spiritual transcendence, unconditional love, and sublime acceptance, to scathing condemnation, incendiary rage, and the deepest despair. Her poetry is always heartfelt and much of it is as raw and direct as a punch to the solar plexus. Heidi does not mince words, and she is utterly devoid of literary pretension. She strings together dazzling declarations, incisive observations, and vibrant imagery with cringeworthy clichés and stock phrases. Her wry, sarcastic sense of humor is both charming and disarming. She is a master of *stream of consciousness* worthy of comparison with James Joyce. Almost anyone can recite their random thoughts at a poetry slam, as Heidi occasionally did, but few can carry it off with such effortless dexterity. One can only marvel at the depth, innate poetic structure, and timeless significance of her seemingly offhanded observations.

Heidi's prodigious powers of physical description are another key element of her unique poetic style. She creates vivid and memorable images in the reader's mind with a few deft verbal brush strokes, much as an artist creates a gesture drawing that captures the essence of a living subject in a few spare lines. Her exceptional kaleidoscopic imagery is often breathtaking, but it is rendered in the service of a higher aim--expressing and conveying her life experiences, her emotions, and her state of being in the world with fierce affirmation, even in the face of despair. Any poet who can articulate all these elements, and employ them so masterfully to engage the hearts, minds, and spirits of her readers, is surely a gifted artist worthy of widespread attention and acclaim.

In many ways, the essence of Heidi Schneider is reflected in the title of this book, *I Am Here But I Am Not*, the first line of one of her last poems, composed about two months before her tragic death from colon cancer on 10 August 2020. Some who knew her intimately describe Heidi as a reluctant soul who incarnated with great trepidation and was never truly at home in this cruelly imperfect world. Nevertheless, over the course of her 34 short years on earth she served ably as a caretaker and a registered nurse, gave birth to two beautiful sons, and lived a full life, all while simultaneously dwelling in the timeless realm of the absolute eternal. For Heidi the veil between these two worlds was always very thin, and that tension is indelibly captured in her remarkable poetry, which has the unmistakable ring of truth and captures both the visceral and the ethereal in a mesmerizing amalgam few other poets can match.

This book commemorates the life and creative work of our precious daughter Heidi Schneider, but it is also a window into her exalted consciousness and the extraordinary poetic gifts that constitute her priceless bequest to the world. I hope that reading it brings you the joy of entering the inner dimensions of a truly remarkable human being, one who sadly had to leave us far too soon.

Sic transit gloria mundi.   Jason Schneider

PRESENTING THE POETRY FOR PUBLICATION

Heidi Schneider was a compulsive poet. She turned out poems at any hour of the day or night and, whenever seized by the creative urge, she'd drop everything and write them down. Unfortunately, she also inherited her father's trait of disorganization, so collecting the scores of poems included in this volume was challenging. They were compiled from the following sources: printouts and handwritten manuscripts kept in folders, handwritten entries in Heidi's journals and notebooks, text files stored on her computers, iPads, and iPhones, and a small selection of poems she posted on Facebook and other social media. I am deeply indebted to Heidi's dearest friends Krista Feichtinger and Gabriella Wolman for sending me a wealth of additional material they had saved on her electronic devices or were accessible in internet posts.

Because of the desultory nature of the source material, and the fact that Heidi hardly ever dated her poems, it is impossible to provide anything like a complete chronology of her work. The dates on computer printouts offer some clues but they are hardly dispositive. The best we can do at this point is to place them in three broad categories—early, middle, and late—based on approximately when they were collected and their general style and content. As a result, we decided to present the poems in this book in no specific order of chronology, content, or style. This gives the reader the opportunity to run through them at random, and to experience the joy of discovery much as we did. The sole exceptions are a small number of Heidi's early poems that appear at the beginning of this book and a handful of late or final poems that we placed near the end.

Since Heidi's primary passion was for writing poetry, and she wasn't focused on creating a literary legacy, preparing these poems for publication proved to be an arduous task. Many of the typed and handwritten manuscripts are replete with misspelled and garbled words that were never vetted or corrected by the author, and most of Heidi's block letter manuscripts (she never mastered cursive script) are barely legible, requiring considerable time and effort to transcribe accurately. There are some notable exceptions—poems that were clearly crafted with great care, and one, "A Poem For Everyone," that she inscribed in "Gothic" characters on fine paper using a calligraphy pen, and then framed. These half-dozen-or-so poems were evidently those intended for posterity—her message to the world.

Transcribing, vetting, and formatting these poems was not a process anyone could have executed perfectly, but I have performed these onerous labors of love to the highest practical standard, based on my intimate knowledge of the poet, her poetry, and her verbal and spelling lapses and eccentricities. In deference to the poet, I have not changed a single word she has written, but I have, very occasionally, made educated guesses when attempting to decipher unclear handwriting or typescript, mostly in cases where simply deleting the ambiguous word was not a good option. To put this in perspective, there are approximately a dozen words in all the poems in this volume that can be called speculative. Finally, in the interest of clarity of expression and cadence, I have made some changes to punctuation and lineation, the way the lines are organized and presented on the page. Like all masterful poetry, Heidi's poems are best appreciated when read aloud, and I urge readers to do so, even for an audience of one.

Our overarching aim in preparing this small volume was to make Heidi Schneider's extraordinary poetry accessible to the widest possible audience, for that is the best way of honoring her blessed memory and her transcendent spirit. We hope that these heartfelt poems will engage your mind and touch your heart.

For Heidi, her sons Nathaniel and Abraham,
and all who cherish her in their hearts.

Heidi's First Poem, Age 11

I know her, yet not.
She is in my dreams
She is Angel Fairylike
With wings of gold,
She cannot listen
to what she's been told
Yet questions it with ever love
so gentle and so kind.
Yet she demands to know
"Is this where God
and heaven lie?
Or is this the road
to trickery and lies?"
She lies back and cries
The eternal question
haunts her,
But she is comforted by
Guardian Angels from above
Yet she knows one thing
as she looks at me
in steady glance
her eyes in ever blue,
"I am not from this world,"
she says,
"I'd like to know, are you?"

Always Raining

Always raining again hard on my car like bullets on tin
in the absence of my presence
such sorrow envelops my being,
suddenly there is the penetrating sound of a car alarm across the
street. Irritation arises. What is the purpose of this irritation?
None whatsoever. Why did you create it? You didn't. The mind
did. It was totally automatic, totally unconscious. Why did the
mind create it? Because it holds the unconscious belief that its
resistance, which you experience as negativity or unhappiness in
some form, will somehow dissolve the undesirable condition.
This of course is delusion.
I grew fat with it, worshiped it
ego completeness sleep and insanity
watching the hours of the clock pass by
I still watch for you
overhead in the distance and the future which never comes
ultimate isolation of my mind which was our mind and yet now
nothing
no thing
unacceptable this pain to me so I witness it in my darkest hours
watch my heart pang
the surrender to this grief comes and goes
I spit mad fire at this dying light
dying of my insides how I looked for that cold hour
where resistance can no longer be sought
pain and this is unthinkable.

Deep Dreams

deep dreams
i'm a waterfall
falling with you
understanding perception--
to fly with butterflies,
uncontrollable
wishes and insight,
laugh--
you itch scabs of pain,
look at my face
to soothe
deep dreams
to blow in pink liquid
pink liquid to inhale,
wander on sunny clouds,
fall with raindown.
i want to kill my separation
float in the void in your head
grow with the grass,
think uncontrollable.
there is no start and no beginning
to wish for life lost,
don't be afraid
to walk through the door.
deep dreams
to be in liquid form,
states of consciousness
like shafts of sunlight,
i do not wish to be human
just perception
walking oddly on useless legs,
apprehension, jerky motion
deep dreams
sleep with green and turquoise,
be your bloodshot eyes
smoke fading with morning light,
it is said:
"we are not a member of society

but a parcel of nature,"
we fight against an invisible world.
deep dreams
to be translucent
to kill thought to think,
to end in a wood
to see dark shadows
to be what we observe
to be emotion, sinking, rising,
i wish to be invisible,
not a consumer
but part of the consumed,
to be bitten like a berry
dissolved in saliva.
what are you?
it takes thought,
compared to what?
how else should i know?
now tell me, make it clear
to be eaten fully
smaller than, less than
a grain or dot
i am being devoured.
deep dreams
to be a nightmare
an afterimage of the sun,
to flow like blood in your veins,
the consciousness, the subconsciousness,
tell me what you want--
"ignorance"
i am
what am i?
i am that i am
what?
the sinking feeling
i am unspeakable,
the dot, the fall, the emotion
to swirl and sink

to purge and replenish
to comprehend
to dive into a deep dream
searching for light
a hundred feet below the surface,
my lungs explode
i have reached my destination
i am coming down.

Sift through these sands

Sift through these sands,
my hands carve bands,
with ink swerves, and curves of words,
for surely what's disturbed,
is same as what does stir,
this whirling dervish dance,
not chance, but stance of stone,
does loan you homes of bone.
and bodies break, no mistake,
your fate is atom crumbling,
energies flight from bumbling,
far from footstep stumbling,
do you hear the rumbling?
science has reported,
that physics is contorted,
all the laws aborted,
for chaos is more sorted,
than the order we hoarded,
lorded over borders
the Lord has all recorded.

So, take a sip of sanity,
the always perfect plan of Thee,
His story is all History,
Nonsense the only sense to me.
Blind are ye, so find the sea
And wash the eye so you might be
The glorious drop of Glory, see?
Simple is the answer how,
All ways lead to always now,
Holy all as holy cow,
When you kneel, God takes a bow.
So Wow all this time
caught up in strife,
Love is why we all have life.

Bad Day

may the 15th-20th
june 12th- 17th

cause i can't fit two with two to make four
it's always like one and a half and 2,
and there's that missing, missing piece
that makes me calculate the angles of my life and fall short
my naked body on the warm bed sheets,
i can feel the beating of my heart as i fantasize
about a world where all the pieces fit together

it's not okay
and it never has been
always contemplating the end,
no, it can't be true
it's the must in the west, the true anarchist
torn like a bloody wound
it's the moment of time and it's not true
and it was like sunday morning or
the first time you heard stairway to heaven or
the soft chilling feel of spring breeze
you said i want to be alone with my disease
where the cracks can't shoot up
the layer of frost burnt my fingers
but still i wandered
past the gravel paths that lead me
home
and i want it to be summer
summer in your lazy arms
sliding past the curves in the road
melting ice cream on my sick lap
and still, i held you to me
like a love song that pieces
and fades

it was like the rumbling of trucks tell you that you were l sat
with your ear
to the pavement

7

with your voice in your throat
and it should be
anywhere but here
this getup these jeans and these hips
this short-sleeved purple shirt
this hair in a ponytail
and it's a rumble of words
like an incoherent sigh condensed with meaning
like my body
spread open and examined for evidence of my soul
female
female
like lace and lip gloss
like braces and bra straps
and i'm holding my crotch
like trying to stop the break, broken energy
it's heaving into the pink blanket
you said blue blanket you
you said "hide under the blue blanket and cut off my curls
hide under the blue blanket so god doesn't know i'm a girl"
but i'm helpless here holding my body up for display
holding myself up on my small
feet and i swear
that heaven is dancing
in my eyes just past your reach and
it's a sickness
the way peanut butter and white bread sticks
to the roof of your mouth, sick shock value

because it's too hard

because it's too hard to look you in the face
i'm looking all down around you baby
like it's too hard to look in the mirror
and it's too hard to use hair spray
because the smell gets to you.
what am i?
a dubious figment of my own imagination
all caught up in drama and supposed woes
sitting in the bathtub past midnight
with the window open...

Poem on an Envelope

I am here but I am not
my heart tried letting go of its grievances
one by one, like letting go of balloons
flying higher until they disappear—

may the space which once I occupied,
by a sweet one be filled—with the things
dearest to me—
Forsythia, gingerbread cookies,
and absolute wonder—

each thing felt in my small body
as infinite as anything could be—
cloudless skies—dusk,
the exult smell of the forest—
lay me down to that

Poetry flowed out of me

Poetry flowed out of me,
dreamed like my bones
helping cracks seeking the pen's slip grip
of my heart,
mad pistol grip facing the end of
sunrises sunsets held in dreamy, suspended air,
to see worlds which tear apart my heart
like existence.
It's like what is this I'm knowing
in this last moment?

put this pussy to your malted liquor lips and still
it burns and somehow
I am sliding in-between the cracks until I can't find myself,
just lost in the atmosphere,
hearing the sounds of city talk in the quiet air
wishing I was there somewhere close to
the brown warm ground.
I watched the wind move the leaves,
tracing the earth with a passion I could never comprehend
this bitter end, sweetly caressing the earth
with my nail polished hand.
lover, I hold your secret in my womb
my strong woman legs
seek grounding to your base
still i swirl in this abstract of celestial being,
seeking, seeking
the breathed in moment of hope when my heart
escapes the constraints of my mind and beats perilously free,
like waves on the shore

the mashed potato death was coming to get me
I could feel it, like a lump in my throat
my sad hollowed out eyes dreamed of bleeding orange sunsets
my numb cold hands traced my face like a blind person
trying to see it's the end
I swear as I stare at the white wall which swims before me
like an ever-changing block to hold myself up against,

my pussy felt like an absent space
that should have been filled-0—

it's the groundbreaking realism
of words which I don't speak,
cast myself into this dark corner that I can't see out of.
I'm scared like when they used to make fun of me
pointing, laughing at my strange clothes,
peanut butter jelly face
like sticks pointing at the village idiot
and I can't seem to expel the notion hidden in me
hidden in me, like a clit under folds of skin to protect me.
it's the warmth of your body but you never seemed to
understand that I literally wanted to fold into you, to disappear,
it's an old story of how sitting on the other side of the bed
with the folded pink covers
I forget which one of us was who,
I looked at the wrinkles of your concerned face
and could not differentiate myself from you,
its' so true I feel like a missing rib walking awkwardly in winter
underdressed and I'm sacred by this
I'm scared by this one step two step onto the concrete sidewalk
that seemed to span
years and tears of my life
the winter sting, hollow on my bold unpretty face
contrasted with moonlight up tight.
and I didn't want this to be true.
Didn't want to feel this, wanted to
be in summer loosely grabbing my breasts pushed to the surface
forgetting myself on rum lips like everything I ever wanted
like everything I ever wanted
and you weren't it, you weren't it
and it's like it's like it's like
days spent in dull contemplation of nights
which helped gray morning in my heart like whispered words
like guys who didn't take me seriously,
wasted still morning gray to take on
my windowless room, hide my stuffy heart in its expanse,
and my words to myself spun
as I stepped out onto the tile floor

of sunspots seeping into my skin,
and my head ached dull with a buzzing that wouldn't quit
with a sound like a jukebox, like the way
the highway spanned out in front of me.
like every morning I could pretend I was running away,
away past the days of self-made prison icons seeping this way,
sleeping this way to the beat and the beat and the beat
of the earth's surface tears.

please, how do I quit?
where is the off button?
and I'm tripping out
and I'm tripping out,
it wasn't right how you were like an arrow
and I was like stretched canvas over wood
with holes I could hold like this.
which seeps from my perilously seeking
the end of this new world order.
order me fries and coke he said
his pretty face, oily glance
and all lay in soapy water.
sad, sad days of hearts which wear too thin
and spin like sunspots moving daily, every day westward
and it seems I will never forget
the setting sun, the cold earth
as my face folded into the sound of wind
howling past the barn
rain like hard pinpricks drenched my skin
I was losing myself, waning
to the sound of new delay day whispered still,
of words which I never spoke

I don't know what to do
with the heat electric pace of my mind
I don't know what to do with this sordid time of love
which stalls and breaks
like alabaster marble on a cold hard surface like
ocean spray, beautiful
like intellectual death
and I can't understand the idea

13

the idea of you, the warmth of please
don't
do
this to
me
I don't
know
what to
do with
myself when
you touch my face, trace my bottom
like increase my heart with your body
hardly seeing, hardly awake.
your big lips breathed words
your tongue makes my legs melt
I can't
seem
to
understand
what to do
I don't know what to do,
please
don't do
this
to
me...

Fuck You

fuck you like the back of my throat stinging fuck you like missed
moments fuck you like broken promises glinting on the floor fuck
you like words stuck in my throat fuck you like interrupted
sentences the shape of words heavy in my chest fuck you like
phone static miscommunication fuck you like drunk "i love yous"
fuck you like a little girl's heart open and still fuck you for not
understanding me
fuck you like smiling constrains
fuck you like smiling constrains, of moments in which you exist
so neatly in real color in my mind
fuck you like spaced out inattention
fuck you like being too embarrassed to tell my friends

fuck you like silence
fuck you like silence
fuck you like silence

fuck you with the open purity of a little girl's heart
fuck you like fuck you like chocolate woman,
ice cream and tears woman
and tearful angry

fuck you like surprise, and i want to say it so bad
fuck you like "ahhhh"

fuck you like "ahhh"
fuck you with all of me that can fit into this little print
fuck you with all I can jam
into these too small hands

fuck me like
fuck me like fuck me like
not being sure of myself
fuck me like

knowing the gravity of my self
the quality of my personhood the depth and coarse matter of
myself

15

real, real looking into your eyes
fuck me like knowing this and denying it
fuck me like wasted talent.

A Poem for Everyone

If I could speak of this,
I would tell you that angels
still brush against you,
whisper secrets so beautiful
it's a wonder you can still,
put one foot in front of the
other. Song of your tears,
you must know that from this
I could contrive a conception
as epic as daybreak. Yes, you
may have been broken in pieces.
but you know that only broken
can you give a piece of yourself
to another. Forgive yourself again.
This is what I want to say, to tell
you you're gorgeous. Always.

music

music,
i still have not seen language's laughter,
and you pour more into my ear.
like lute and lyric, you rattle my sanity,
soft shimmers my sight misses.
you spell emotions to my senses,
i rock in note enchantment
as you slip covers loose,
poured again i roll slowly
into your sound sheets,
wrapped by your thighs of sighs and song,
i'm gone.
how could i say in speech
what you build in dream vibration?
let me love you,
and your horns and harps,
your orchestra, loud and silent,
conductor and chaos.

Dunno

When the days are long and waste away at the corners,
days bled out like lines of hope smothered by fear,
I'm hearing the beat, beat of my heart
alarming quiet to my words that quicken and twitch
and I pace myself around
spinning at the simplicity, the common breath,
the sun glittering on the white snow.
the shadows of my life pass me by
pass before my hairs, and I smile.
everything I ever wanted like a stab at desire.
and am I worthwhile?
been better than this blessing close to you across the room
and you caught my eye
I knew by the thump, thump in my heart that you were
something,
got lost in the angles of your face, the complicating measure in
which you bless words to the page
my eyes searing hot as you touch your hands to my lips
your lips brush against mine
and it's like falling butterflies of everything,
everything will end in my demise

For Some Reason

for some reason
i'm such a bore
just a twenty dollar whore
who sells herself like lemonade
at every fucking convenience store

~love is my inspiration but to you it seems to be just as fleeting as
every other good emotion that i feel

yeah, cough up candy corn
i'm all sweet with devil horns
let's list the reasons that you like me
fructose
artificial flavoring
and blue dye #2

blue baby bubble gum
it's so fun
to chew me up and spit me out

baby blue bubble gum
chew me till i'm flavorless and stiff
and spit me out-
i knew you'd never swallow
cus once you've licked my sugar coating off
there's just
nothing left to do.

Girl in the Parking Lot

The words have perfect
When I scribble words in book that
Describe her, this girl. Twist me and
Swirl these feelings inside way too big
To hide behind my smile when she
Smiles. Brain Calculates. Insane mouth
Cannot make the connection. Lose
My heart in convection, no protection
From tongue ties--I try to untie
With all of my might, discuss on the
Sidelines what I must pull from my
Throat. Take note. I'm about to choke.
Is it better that I stutter, mumble and Mutter?
What language do I speak
to ask for her number? Blibbidy blah
paling language stalls and gives her
my number instead as a chorus yells
in my head, "write her name down.
Hide E's in the alphabet. Are your
teeth drunk?" did I have too much
punch? I crunch and munch on
the words dripping from my head
like soggy bread. Dive in fog, never
stop and pause 'cause I've been
pulled into her aura. I'm new. She's
new. Maybe we two could speak truths
over a bottle of YooHoo. "I'll see
You later" She made me lose sleep.
All I could do was think, listen to
My speak in waking dreams
about the most beautiful spirit I've
Ever seen. What color were her jeans?
Her Shirt? Her hair? Her eyes? I would
Lie if I said I remember. Take me
to November whenever I think of
her smile 'cause, all the while, all
I saw was her smile. So bright
I would startle.

It Was Years Before I Realized

it was years before I realized that nothing would take it away
the little me who put flowers on her blonde hair,
lilacs, and wondered at the dimming sun
beautiful over the house that grew to silhouette, and I wondered
at memories which stand out to me like beings,
like lilies of forget-me-not breaths on the looking glass of night
shock so true, getting washed clothes to cool my burning body on
hot July nights, when I leaned to the buzz of cicadas and the
moon shone just for me,
just through my small, flawed window.

the first time I tasted you, you tasted like hot harsh of everything
I never wanted to remember but stood out in my window like
towers of dreams I used to try to recall,
notebook pressed in my hands.
the shadow of mid-morning lips slashed across my face,
when does trauma happen?
I breathed tremulously
and clasped in your sweet arms and remember
the lilacs of my gramma's garden, wandering along the
perimeters of the cut grass looking for faeries
that I swear I saw
like when I hit my head too hard and saw sparks.
I saw angels dance around me like a promise,
me in my too big sweatshirt and scabbed knees.
do you know me,
me collapsed in your sweet arms? and i'm trying to tell you i'm
trying to tell you through this stupor who i am
something I should know like the back of my hands
but somehow eludes me,
set like bliss kisses in the street
the roads I weaved around to try to find you
listening to anyone, and somehow
I swear this makes sense.

it was so good, like pancakes in the morning drenched in syrup,
rising in the morning to your face,
but the house echoed with an emptiness

that left me banging on the windows, sighing so harsh like the
lashed open air couldn't repeat or hold the vibration of my voice,
couldn't stand the end of this

it was years before I realized that it wouldn't ever go away, never
never never, just like the sky holds the stars the world holds my,
holds my spirit, and then my body and then I swear
when I see flashes of images, images that I had forgotten, a
million sunrises that I slept through, and I beg you
touch me like i'm a person like you're a person and it's the beat
beat it's the beat beat that's fading, endlessly losing its colors like
autumn leaves that die so brilliantly gold, hold the last of your
breaths I ever knew.

I never knew you as a person not a thing
and I'm thinking of the trees planted in lines along the highway,
the way skyscrapers loom,
I'm thinking of the sweetest thing, calling you the sweetest thing
until you die breathless in my hands as morning fades to night,
eyes which turn cold and still were dancing above the gray of city
traffic along with the men
with top hats
and it's a vibration, I never never knew that it would
never stop buzzing
because when you touched, you you shocked my soul
and that can't be put like you weaved over with embroidery to
decorate and conceal the true, like broken bride lights
shining in the dark smothers beautiful faces
before she said I do
it slides in and out of my aging mind and maybe someday
someday i'll understand
wasted still, still so and still I can't come to a conclusion
just as my heart breaks, I hold myself whole
in my bed alone at night,
I hold my self together sewing sewing back the pieces of heart
that were extracted

in the mall I gripped my heart and told you
that sometimes it starts beating too fast or too slow
and it feels like everything has died

and I too would fling myself off this banister
to try to find the hollow wind of light tunnels.
it was so good—
step, step, step,
on the cold wet street and I try to recall…

Crazy #2

the sun set red over half forgotten spans of highway
the days that i break apart my bread cast
apart from the world
up light and seeking some confirmation to my life.
love in July, your hands covered mine like a promise
my shaved head sweating in the sunshine
blue eyes careless in the breeze
you said, "this disease has me,
it's the cold growing at the far end of my mind,"
this despair that would leave me
weeping in the passenger seat
listening to Eric Clapton

the cold autumn leaves hitting the dashboard,
rain poured down
me in a sleeveless shirt
quiet in the rain and breathing
the soft cold air
the wet damp
space of grass where we sat
the sound of the clock ticking, the cold wood floors
your breath like a silhouette all around me
as the sun dies,
its breathless mustard of a
world which i end in a heartbeat—
and still the world,
and still the world holds me
lightness shines through dark alleyways in Febuary
under valentine pink skies
words break hearts apart
witlessness

the sun explodes itself again
i have no words to comprehend it,
and so, i sit motionless as the sun dies
under a moonless sky
its gray steel love all-encompassing shadows.

and the Devil asked

and the Devil asked how badly
do you want it? the thing
that I could bandage your soul?
but holy hell this wound still
weeps, still seeps substances
you could not believe,
I tried to consummate but
the only fate I could,
I could muster was
the one already placed
in me, but this light speaks,
says baby – the world
is filled with things unreal,
but you are not one of them,
you belong to me.
and each time you memorized
the exact color of the sky
I was watching you,
your breath is mine,
the air in your lungs is mine
and is golden like falling stardust.
behold, you are so much more
dressed in human clothes,
your conception was designed
and destined—each flaw
placed with love and intention,
And this is the road we walk,
pretending that destiny didn't
spark whatever this is.
I know that—this moment,
and chaos, and it shows...

The process of un-doing

i want to sit here
in this closet,
as life passes me by
without meaning.
i want to sit here
in this enclosed space
for eternity,
with no fear,
no hope,
no memory.
--i willingly accept
numbness.
i want to lie here
as pictures form
in front of my eyes
telling me of misfortune,
And i want to experience
no empathy.

Don't love me

Don't love me
Don't try to feel
The white hot ache
Of my pain,
Don't try to comprehend
the meaning
Of when I smile
and look down,
Don't brush the hair
out of my face,
Don't memorize my eyes
As they change.
I am a continent
Misplaced
Deep in my self
Swimming miles away,
I only wreck,
So take this day
To not love me.

Blah

let me take pain and
break it until
you can't seem to dwell,
oh hell darling
oh hell i wished the end of me
was lit like the tip of cigarette ashes
mashed to the ground to smother
in its own intensity
watching the whitewash of the fingerpainted iowa sky
like numb over grief of mine
which spills in my eyes and makes my touch
soft and gentle, surreal baby
surreal like a promise i tried so hard to keep
keep myself from imploding into
dull words and emotions that don't convey me
and i'm naked, shaking at the words which swim
oh darling
oh darling
oh oh
darling and i can't stop, can't stop
can't seem too far away from here
i'm pacing to the end of my rope.

you said it was like Newports and coke
they just feel together,
like summer and running naked through a field
like kissing and tears like oh oh girl please
like i wanted to wash
wash my body like i could find the origin of me,
do you know
the intensity of me?
o you know the words which spill
she said darling honey baby please,
please don't please please don't lash out at me
conquer the soul in my breath, the sense of me,
me me, cut like grass like stale flowers
and it goes together like the wandering street
to my house

nearly and almost finding myself again,
it goes together like tuna and car trips,
like bikinis and beaches, wishes wanted, the soul stuff
like butter spread on bread i spread my sick story
down the front of my shirt.
like spilled food i couldn't control
it broke out of my mouth
like stale promises, like wasted over hope
like nothing like nothing like nothing
that i could like, nothing that i could seek,
like the expansion in my dead flowers,
and i don't want it i don't want it
i don't want it to be true
true like washed over and wasted,
like soul crushed and expanding
to a death, like a death, like a death sentence.

girls walking home

sadly
sung
to the chill october air
resonating each amber leaf with a story
of girls walking home from school
their soft straight hair
against their pretty cheeks
one step in front of the other
until they find
some destination

COKE

because you don't understand like brandy on hot july nights
when you bend to the steam and melt into the music, the beat
which dissolves sweet and bitter
yes, and know on the pain in which you hover takes flight,
like a bird in autumn and you speak silence. do you,
do you want to try some?
I paused. I felt the heat on my face
and quiet like the way my top lip curled to the buzz of the room
"yes"
and he smiled
and said it's okay girl, we'll just give you a bump
a bump?
Yes, a bump
razor blades and perception

The windows from heaven

The windows from heaven
The doors alive
In this great world
    of unknown,
For the sky doth kill
on an Autumn day
The bird is silenced
        forever.
In that moment
    the tear alive,
Swelling, swelling, till it drops
Bringing the flower to life
    Yet killing creation.

That one tear of your pain,
the pain you held for so long,
A single tear, a single tear
Your eyes are red,
but to blink a few,
Hiding the sadness within
Until it overflows.

Then go there, go there
The gates of heaven open,
They bring you in with gladness,
They were alive then,
Beckoning, beckoning,
You saw them there before.
The bird is yet again
    Conscious
  Sad for it wishes
When will you take it
        oh death
In that tear that seems
        Forever.

Free Flow

All your fear all your ambition all your hope
all your intuition
flung upward into the swirling sky by and by
to crash and crumble rumble with
the imperfection of it.
The sore back shadow of everything
that you are holding
being too much, the devastation of the last fall down
and I can't explain the white sky shutter, the lost prospects of a
dream that you had, that is lost
and I feel like I can't let go of it

it's the heartbreak kid and I can't control myself
to think of anything better,
it's lying awake and tossing and turning and thinking,
of then the feeling of the sheets and the crumbs
and your heart's slow rhythm
think of all your contradictions
and the things you do that make it hard
to look into your eyes,
all this dismiss this heartfelt, nonsense emotion
overwhelmed by clear eyes on a Sunday morning
all this life thing this life feel caught up in your throat,
like how the road felt,
he said he said "I've been tasting roads"
the way the trees felt, the spaced-out realism
of being high
and not being able to explain the cold feeling,
of trying to fuck up to make it better
even though it makes no sense.
the heartsick burdened feeling of knowing and feeling
like nothing could ever be beautiful again
eating ice cream bars in the car trying to make it better but
failing, miserable failure. I drove past the house where it all
happened
the light on the wood floor, the curve of the wall
to the bathroom
my blood on the toilet seat

that you made me wipe up,
getting lost in aisles of aisles of food
in the grocery store.
Staring at my breasts in the mirror
at your family's house
staring at the red fabric that I didn't quite feel out.
What do you do with the past?
What do you do with it?

the spaced-out detached realism of being high,
when you're not the destructive, compulsive, eating, shopping,
smoking, drinking, talking on the phone because because because
that moment of space, of feeling your heart shudder, lost in your
chest,
is too much to bear, and i fling myself at the drive-through into
other people, problems question my heart and tear at my eyes,
i stare at the curves
of my body like some sort of—painting,
not hoe like some actress, but female and whole
but i'm still rolling like it's gone,
like my heart sank into the sea without me
i can't and i don't know what i'm trying to say
it's over, it's gone,
the sun shines half assed onto my face
but somehow fails and leaves darkness in its place.
around the world is gray to me
matter is matter-less, and careless
and still i'm uncontrollable
like a bloody kiss, neatly burnt on my heart
i don't have the resource to start over
haunted by the dark trees in august,
 haunted by your dream
and still feeling, in retrospect,
never speak their true meaning to me.
what i'm i trying to say i'm so scared of
this prophesy of love
and you can't have me...

i always have a story to sell

i always have a story to sell
hell
i could be night trippin'
in my own apartment sitting
and i can talk to the fucking walls man
tell them who i am
feel the sound disappear into the plaster
faster than i can speak
you all know it's not weak
you all tell me so,
like i don't know
like i haven't been there for you
like i haven't wandered these streets
desolate, breaking my conscience
over the park bench where i lay
like i haven't...
sold my soul for love
gotten down in the dirt, grass stains on my shirt
walked barefoot on the pebbles and burrs
just waiting man, just watching
'cus i can't see any tomorrow,
and yesterday has disappeared into a haze
of lost ideals
and promises that break in my hands
when i examine them
so i sit, stomach sick
just waiting for some sort of calm.

Don't deny the early wish

Don't deny
the early wish,
the wish of light
until the dark.

talking to her
in your head
it's a mistake
or just an accident
Zion? Zion?
Hmm this is it.

I know what you think—
it's a real world
you stuck in the door.

Crap

the end of words which sit in my throat
and fester like the dank result of death
the end of the fucking end of the world
the fucking end of the world
and it's the fucking end of the world—

i weighed myself against the moon,
i took two straight steps past the moment
which i cast in the moonlight,
heavy in the light
as the winds and gravity of the world
help up my heart for you to taste—

i weighed myself against the moon,
moonlight falters
bright patches of light like flashes of insight
that weigh heavy, heavy in my heart,
like the quiet stirring of a river
winding endlessly down toward some end—
why and why?
and how can you ask for passion without,
without insanity?
it's the, it's the, it's the, it's the, it's the
ennnnnd of the world
like strawberries in fall
like kisses missed,
the heart and soul holding
like i wish i could seep through the cracks,
the cracks like nonsense
on the back of my tongue like cock,
because you can't stop the beat
the beat you can't stop you can't stop the beat
you can't stoooooooooooooooooooooooooooop
the beat—
let strawberry death
as sweet and serene
as sun girls bathing in the afternoon sun
perfect body big tits on a skinny girl,

we all wanted skinny death like
the half-assed moon
splintered and shining
in the dull plastic sky,
what do you want to do
skinny death?
squirm like a sick chest
a sick chest like words
which hollowed out the space in my heart
like parasites,
and you can't have the
dusty sunlight spaces in my heart which dwell in
mid-summer afternoon
along with the buzz of cicadas
bent over angel of death,
bent over

through the ocean's cold embrace

through
the ocean's cold
embrace water plays
with light and days
waste away in happy thoughts
And words dissolve on tongues too
sweet And shadows dance with fading
day. Oh i have wasted myself
in numb embraces.

Bar

and it's like this dirty bar
and me hazed up still so I can't feel,
I should be torn, but my emotions are far away or so it feels lost,
and the sound of this creeps past my mind and I'm drowning in
this sea of faces mouthing words, and I'm laughing with the
rhythm of the music and it comes back, to the back my hips are
swaying
you smile, and I say I don't want you

who am I to you? Who am I to me? And is it okay, the things
that I do? And I smile and pinch your arm,
look you in the face and laugh at the way
this all goes down
write about it, sex, this thing i can't explain
i'm humming the words and the music is playing,
and if it didn't hurt and if it didn't mean anything
and involve awkward glances,
long shower and regret
i would want you to want you to have me,
and i can't help but think about your shoulders
and think about the way your hand would feel
sliding down my waist.

Flowers wilt

Flowers wilt
with embraces too cold to feel
and i thought i was abandoned
and i thought you didn't hear

i wish i didn't have to prove
to you
my fragile heart was breaking
and i looked at the world
and was forsaken

all was forsaken, and everything,
beings seeing
and child's eyes
looked at the wonder, and fell to the ground pleading
take it away,
won't you
take it away
melt it like jelly in your mouth.

So all the world
turned to liquid
and fell from your eyes
and you apologized

seeing city blocks and chalk
your hands too delicate to touch our faces
too cold to cease the crude choking
or stop the bleeding or hear hearts beating.......

Taking it away:
the world would dim like night falling ever so slowly
the world would begin to break
and you, crying, would take it away

like wind spilling from the north in gasping heaves
you would delete
you would delete
swiping our memories and turning them to dust.

hunt

let this feeling stop—
my moment of weakness,
passed out on the floor and exposed,
the way my heartbeat told you
of the way the dying trees
felt in warm decay,
the quiet, numb pause
when your heart rises above your mind
and you can witness beauty,
the sad lament of humanity,
the tears, the soft blood spilling in excess,
as if it could prove anything.
i witness this, my womanhood,
the soft vulnerability
that requires your good consciences
this shadow of my doubt,
this delay of my reaction.
you can see this advantage you have—
that i require your good consciousness.

Someone asks: A Romance

Someone asks, "why do you not drink?"
Do they not see it in my eyes?
I am drunk off your very breathing,
Your footsteps always land
on the door knocker of my heart,
When it opens your lips pour wine over my soul.
I am swimming, intoxicated in you,
The swimming just makes me drunker.
I say silly things and forget my schedule.
That's ok, it's only filled with you anyway.
∞
People think i'm crazy,
If only they knew they would lock me up.
I'm a love terrorist,
I will not stop till the world is slain with love.
You did this to me,
Filled my heart with crazy notions,
Gave me art as weaponry,
And unlimited ammo from my soul.
∞
You think this is about God?
My love Poetry?
It is, but it is not mine,
it is yours,
and it is about You.

i want to make you breakfast,
warm pancakes to the lips of your plate,
Tap my heart,
And give you syrup of my love.
∞
Does this love scare You?
Then run, for it is just beginning,
It is sunlight ever sent,
and caught between two mirrors.
They cry with glassy sweat from the heat,
Always excited about the returning beam!

Don't fool yourself anymore,
You know more than your education,
There was no learning this truth,
It's the one that made the teacher.
You feel it?
Twisting in the coils of knowledge,
Sweep out the fear shavings,
So it can dance in innocent bewilderment.

∞

What is happening?
Do not ask me,
I am looking like the driver,
And being dragged around by my Heart.
You make me write this,
I cannot even slow my pen,
My handwriting bounces sloppily
          here and there,
Never knowing where it's going next.
Once in a while it stops,
For my pleading hand aches and cries,
"I am not built to hold this Love,
     give me rest, so I may try
          to sail with You."

∞

Do you know?
I so often wonder what secrets you hide
Under your skirt and eyelids,
Like cookie jars to my soul.
Don't mistake this for lusting,
I never want your cookies for myself,
I want to draw them out of hiding
and share their steaming sweetness with you.

Don't say you don't believe me,
I don't believe myself,
I'm pouring out of a bottle,
Into a cup of You.

This talk is insanity,
The way each drop of me laughs in ripples,
as it lands welcomed with the rest,
encompassed in your holding.

I have no better way,
none worse as well,
it is nonsense to sing of You,
you are the song itself.
Don't think this is not You here,
That You can read Yourself on this Page,
It was You before You wrote it,
You just wrote my heart to send it.

∞

I bet you wonder at times,
Sitting in the small confines of fear,

"This cannot be for me,
  It must be for someone else.
  This writing is love for God,
   I do not reflect these
   great metaphors"

Do I need to answer?
Must I say your name,
That's maybe what you want,
Will that convince you
That you were on my mind
as each pen stroke wrote itself?

Call me crazy again,
Already in Love with You.
Reading the notes of your Heart,
Only to see they're beyond me.
Listen how these words care for you,
You fool yourself to think they aren't,
Now hear me whisper your name.
I'm caught in your cloak again,
Crumpled in your pocket.

It doesn't matter to me,
My heart bought this ticket,
I'm just along for the ride.
∞
People get so scared of Now,
Later they come back yelling,
    "I didn't know."
Fools,
There is no knowing,
Leave that to the scholars,
We that are blinded by Love
Should feel our way around.
        ∞
You are the market to me,
Fruits I never heard of,
Spices my stomach loves to
    torture itself with,
Flowers, swinging in the hands of ladies,
The crowd, the noise, the battle of color,
Chaos without you,
You make it art.

That falafel was my heart,
How quickly you devoured it,
But i put some aside,
Just a small piece,
Enough for eternity.

No, I can't read your mind,
Sometimes you sing it to me quietly,
But it is always you
that reads it to me.
        ∞
I once rode in a bumpy yellow chariot of Love,
Perhaps it was the sun,
Visiting, disguised with a little rust,
You were there next to me,
Singing into the stars,
Your hair dancing with the wind.

I swallowed my heart with your notes,
They've been digesting together since.

The longest rose I ever knew,
Couldn't bear not to be with You,
It stayed a rose to smell your fragrance,
And petal by petal,
Surrendered to your beauty.

∞

Every now and then,
When my heart and stomach talk,
I taste rice and peppers,
Mushrooms and onions,
Soft sweet lips, and warm polenta.

How I dislike the bristles of my beard,
But for whatever reason,
I only shave it with you.

Why is it that I so love to dance?
It is when my heart gets the reins to my body,
It turns me like a puppet,
Laughing wildly the whole time,
Sometimes a little proud about the eyes
                on its puppet show,
But that is never the prize,
For every once in a while
You stand up and dance with it.

∞

I took a pill once,
It was supposed to make me perfectly happy.
I should have known
That it would make me think of you.

The memory of You paints pictures and portraits
                in my seeing,
The likes of which shame the great artists,
Yet every time You are present,
I toss them back in my mind like cheap postcards,
Realizing the dull copies against the Original.

49

∞

You make me want to be a Thief,
I think of stealing the Words of great Lovers,
I want to shower you in Shakespeare,
Waltz you in Whitman,
Roll you in Rumi.
How silly when I realize
I already have.

This loving is to be taken lightly,
With the understanding of its depth.
It is like swimming in milkweed feathers,
In a basin of the stars.

∞

I tell myself no more forgetting,
Still, it happens time and time again,
And then all of a sudden,
I remember You,
And my thawing heart undresses.
Who knows if I'll throw its coat away,
It's so nice to come back to you.

It seems my body can not take this,
This outpour of Love for you,
But even when I drop my pen to rest it,
My heart sings and dances on,

I am pummeled by the soft fists
            of Your Love,
Are your hands sore from my hard shell?
Sometimes I do not see the cracking,
Other times, I am fit to shatter.

∞

We write together,
There is no need to separate,
This hug of oneself.
Our love is union,
Rain drops ocean landing.
The sunlight and the sun,
The two is made from one.

We fly, soaring in mind rockets,
Bright shine off the coats of clouds
Drops our eyes to quiltwork patches.

∞

This curling net of ideas,
Sprouting from our head like ivy fighting,
What story will it tell today?
That is beauty fooling,
Twists of trickery,
Saying silence and slow in growing.
This net of needle-less nettle,
Playing dead these moments,
A testament to us.

How we're writing silliness,
Love's kiss we are,
And its story more.

∞

I wash windows to your Love,
And fog them with my breath again.
I drop my rag and cry,
You press your lips against the pane,
You laugh at me in your kisses,
I close my eyes and sleep in your laughter.
Suddenly, this sleeping is really waking.
There is no window,
Just our glassy reflection
at the edge of our eye.

I try to write about You,
How is it to describe infinity?
Why do I have to tease myself,
There is no solving this puzzle,
It never runs out of pieces,
I keep finding flat edges to be a border,
But I haven't made a side.
You're ticklish with sexual laughter
as I fondle and stir Your pieces.

51

Maybe I don't want to win,
Playing seems more the prize.
                    ∞

I apologize if I Love You too much.
Maybe You want me Home,
But I'm sometimes afraid,
If I come back
How will we be Loved?

Sometimes you shake me like a drink.
I get drunk off myself,
And stumble into the night,
Singing of a great Love
That turned the stars into wine drops.
Some people think me mad and smile,
But this is just our thinking,
It's really us,
Laughing at our crazy Love,
And smiling through our distant teeth.

Say how can this be,
No way to see it and everywhere I look
                    there it is.
We get lost in our beauty with no mirror,
Devotion has got us lost,
Now devotion will have to draw the map.
                    ∞
We talk about Going Home.
This is the babble of those sick with knowledge,
We never left and we never started,
We sit in the middle of that with no sides.

Who's signing their name on every atom?
Those circles seem to be the first name,
Yet in them is another signature,
The original is the one that keeps on going.

How many forms you have chosen,
and my incompetent fingers

aching to fondle the truth.
There are secrets you have that sex borrows,
Lust steals your blossoms,
And dances like a bird with attractive feathers.
The vastness in the kiss is closer to you.

∞

Again, i dream of you in waking moments,
Blue eyes i can cry for.
When i laid between your legs,
My heart shivered in fear.
It whispered how it wished to sleep inside you,
Then it remembered,
How to be within you, it was truly awake.

Haunting how we share nothing, still,
This love is pouring.
Why do i drown in you,
A stone rounded and willing,
Laying in your riverbed?

What a heavenly sin if that,
to spill myself into your cup
to lay my liquid love within your goblet's rim.
trimming your hair's toss with my breath,
it is the dance of your neck against my lip,
when, like a flask, fallen drunk into
          a full glass of wine,
we drip together in thick, sweet swirling.
i ponder your legs like vines around mine,
          to taste your jaw and twists.
I might eat your form like heavy mist,
          lunging against my mouth.

∞

Spent time wandering with her,
Broken feet from forgetting my steps,
We stopped, and watched
A seedling's spiral fall...
     wings that whistle to the small and virtuous,
     drumming vegetable feathers,
     troubling the thoughtful stillness of the water.

53

Her rainbow shoes carried my feet,
Rotted rubber, was more an angel chariot to me,
Where is their walking now?

I cannot involve her in this madness,
She would faint of sheer exhaustion
From all the dancing in my heart.
I watch the loveliness of her wrist,
Now her hand, like a dreaming lady
Is led in the wake of her hips,
Her smile that pulls shadows along her cheeks,
And she spins in scarves of my watching.

Again, i couch myself in memories,
This simple happiness has sailed,
i feel cursed by this green land,
a thief masked in wet grasses,
smiling hills like green Tara's breasts,
holding the prize i cannot win.
                    ∞
What seeps into my watery eyes,
Vibrant color,
Settles into my seabed pupils,
as a ship slow sinking.
          the sights of you are worse than blinding,
          like long stares at the sun,
          you burn your glowing figure,
          a love stamp on my hungry retina.
where lies this painter you?
exuding puppet drops of color,
the image of your beauty,
frozen paint explosion,
liquid hyacinth blossom orgy,
folding of shifting color fabrics.
you are organized oil drops,
in the rippling puddle of my eye.
you are the gearworks of fascination,
a stain glass melting round fire.
if you could see for a moment,

the true beauty that you are,
you would devour yourself,
like a bee and nasturtium honey.

∞

who chooses my words with such intricacy?
i have not the notice of such infinite sublimity,
subliminally transposed on life's picture screen.
grey dream gone gay and light slopes play,
as kaleidoscopes pray for lookers.
this looking glance of focus,
stance and forgetting we're standing,
is energy gift wrapped and slapped
in your heart's box?
just a white lipped lamp,
stamped with a ring of hands of all colors,
fingers in beckoning rainbow dust.
fine sheets of unsewn silk that follow not the wind.
aura of my misunderstanding,
my passing of light in a peacock flurry,
silent and spherical collage,
garnishing the dimples of the moon.
clouds surf the glow garland of her head,
round splintered diamonds,
hovering, like static shavings in the sky.

∞

God, how You bake me in temptations of your beauty,
You arrive, swollen and flushed pink,
Soft lips shawl over your firm jaw.
You have curves i always follow,
Breasts i wish to toss my tongue about,
Paint you in the pressures of my kiss.

I feel the tightness build in my body,
this passion food i feed myself,
these dream raptures of your sweetness.

red hairs sway on your arched neck,
your hips rise against my fingers,
how i play on the soft instrument of your sex,

meet your melting with my mouth,
catch moans in my cupped hands,
motions of my spiraling tongue in you,
twists of your thigh bottoms,
wrestling with the strength of my shoulders.
then to lift and lay myself into you,

plough you in love's roughness,
hard toss to part your thighs,
and grappling my push inside,
your warm cry on my neck,
the turn of your hips against me,
your sex aching around mine,
ravenous for the next sweet thrust.

my hard palms spread wide under
the small of your back,
grabbing you up into my fierce digging,
lap your breasts in wetness,
as your muscles wander under me,
oblivious, each taut form of you
moaning and laughing on its own,

as the pressure and our lunging together
shatters the electricity of your nerves
into sparkling ice particles
you feel melting down the inside of your thighs,
till in my last deep throbbing,
we spill liquids together
to run warm drippings soothing your flesh,
and we slip together into the sleep
of each other's orgasmic warmth.

Crazy #1

sick spattered on the cold tile floor
i have suffered the atrocity of sunsets
the cold stream on my sick feet
the lost day that i spun out of control
woman holding the world, the dearth of myself
in beautiful crimson and gold unfolding
until i be let go in a breath
and the world and the world
banished from my sight the last day of July.
i was driving down the highway
the street disappearing from my view
faster than can imagine
i flew past sunset rest, i was
weaving my whole world behind.
you said you loved him
cus he was the only one
who closed his eyelashes
to see if he could see rainbows through them
the cold stream that i traveled to
my feet on the pavement
my head wrapped up in scarves
like an old Russian woman
i said i was just traveling through
and this delight was more
than i could ever ask for
like fog on a windowpane
i drew stories for you that you couldn't comprehend
like in the back seat
driving through Spring Valley
i would write my name backward so the
Hassidic Jews could see,
later you told me
that they wouldn't talk to me because my
arms where bare, bare to pick up
the sun spiraling down
over half eaten falafel
and wordless love

i Had seen it all before
" i loved you before i knew you"
-Jeremiah 1:5
I had miscarried before and
a teenage girl who
shed stale blood tears onto
ratty old sweatpants
dreamed about you under cold sunsets
my grief laying in like calm waters
and still when I had you
I expelled you
cramping on the bathroom floor
screaming as the cold winds of March
wreaked havoc on the leftover leaves
and still I sit here
my pussy sore and used
feigning half sleep on sickbed covers
where useless exchanges
happened under the waning moon,
and I'm afraid
at the whole horrid vaporous quality
of the memories which outline my mind
leaving me praying for blood
despite my love.

find me a home

find me a home for i'm houseless and lost,
tossed from your balcony for thinking
        there was an edge to you.
did i not love you like your heart,
was i not the drop of your wave,
        hold me in your crashes?
am i no longer longing for the
        sea spray's leap,
        no longer asleep?
wake me in your circling tide pool,
let me escape into your vastness,
let me be your feast and not your hunger.

What are you trying to say

What are you trying
to say when you can't make
it elegant anymore?
Because words and images
pour until you quit this
feeling wordless, like a
hole in the soul that's
bleeding no matter what i
would tell you.
something beautiful like
words hold me down
eaten by grief's memories
of what feeling only silent,
that a river that has run dry
and you don't respect me.
my voice quivers in the aftermath
you see the word order only,
in my eyes and not in my heart
which has stumbled over
silence and remained frozen
only to see you—
poetry has left me dry
and wordless
holding onto something
i stopped trying to explain
and i have become so logical
i see only in words
that fit together like a puzzle...
why am i here,
what is the point of me
if not to express something?
he hurts me,
and talks of memory,
And he dismisses, like
apple cores.

slit my wrists

slit my wrists the best i can
and I'll always be that to you, a slit with broad hips
misplaced eyes and a
heart for you to eat,
toward the end i'll rearrange my name
swear i never loved you
smile at myself in the mirror
and be gone far above my head
while my body twists and shakes
and i'll pretend i can't feel
silly nerve ending
pain is for lesser creatures, animals caught in traps
cows forced to eat each other's feces
industrialization, industrialize my heart
make it more convenient
Disconnect it from my body and see?
I'm perfect for the modern world
hitting hard against the turquoise sky
spelling out my pain for you.
i told her
told her i
had been there
shaved head and skinny arms
soulful eyes to protect me
just because you can't understand the eccentricities, the subtle
emotion of women
just because the world is not to you what it is to me
does not mean i am crazy
my body holds more
holds more grief
my tears sting not just for me
but for this female tragedy in silhouette against the winter sky
the numb loss of children, lovers, husbands,
friends rape death
speaks to me through my body
you said it was stale water
in my pelvis unshed tears brewing brown murky pain
with no sound, given no sound

61

how to get past the numb of it
the anesthetic compulsive tendencies that I have
not to feel,
it feels like a bruise like being slapped awake
it's just so hard so hard to take
loss like this I said there is no place for it
not in this world where everything is headed
toward that linoleum equilibrium
that can only mean death
but nature knows better
knows how to die crack and break

mourns the loss of each leaf
the cycle of nature
the cycle of me
knowing, knowing how to grieve
are you really surprised then
that this isn't my home
that this was never mine, that I could never feel right
staring at your white coat with my legs spread open
or sitting across a desk from you as you listen
and try to calculate,
isn't the whole world trying to tell you
how I feel?

Because this is fucked up

The air was thick
it was half conscious air stirred thick
alien thick and hot
exploding this sinew
the hot sun breathless on my skin
cast cast down
into this greasy air
thick hot wanting wishing
like this frozen field
i'm picturing Mary Daily field
sinking into the ground
the hot taste of you
of adulthood
of beer cigarettes
and confusion
I stare at my transparent frame
looking through myself like glass shattering
and I can't explain
the pinpoint of my pain
I said it was hot and thick and suffocating
like the breathless sun
undone child, undone
tearing at my eyes like swollen water
murky brown
heartstrings wound too tight
white hot night
shake growing uptight
I'm bent and i can't control these
shattering wordless,
still like the moonlight on a dusty windowsill
this child thing
this thing I'm mourning I can't explain
the sweetness of the forest
I'm looking for myself down this road
leading nowhere
the shivering goosebumps
this hot ache spit apart pain that remains un-named
split open soul your hands unfolding on my skin

akin to breaking
you broke me open with your touch
wind shivering hot
and I couldn't, couldn't explain
I'm trying to explain the way the road turns
I'm trying but I can't
and I've lost myself somewhere
and I can't seem to get myself back
and I can't mourn the loss
because there's no body, no funeral
and I want to disappear into the darkness
and I want to disappear
into the criss-crossing of branches.

4 haikus

#1
hope is shivering in summer
　　and pollen on your nose
unclose the power of paradise.

#2
　　twilight in mid-winter
to think we could all dwell
　　　　in such beauty.

#3
　　rain fell on hardened slush
　　　i know all the pieces
　　　　　fit together.

#4
　　　eat mangoes by the beach
feel the thump of the ocean life,
　　　　and all this.

He said you look pretty

He said you look pretty in a kitchen
Humble love
Like apple pie

He said you're pretty like pot roast
not like tiramisu
He said you're beautiful like a flower,
like something that grows
But you're not sexy like a car

Maybe I'm something akin to the earth
Necessary and dark
Warm like comfort, something you
remember when you fall asleep...

Freak out

choked like so many thoughts
too many inhales of this cigarette grief
writes its story across your eyes
like a backdrop of Annapolis
twisted cold hands that cling to mine
everything i don't want to remember
the laminate of city buses
Jordan's slack mouth
the warm smell of your brown flesh
the quiet hum of thinking about
the possibilities of life
before everything got sorted into corners
star breath
lightly exhaled
to the soft cold July air
the feel of wet grass
trench coats and rain
the warm smell of sweat...

not to romanticize
I still carried my pain around like a story
how far could I walk in this direction? stepping over
grass growing out of the cracks in sidewalks
summer was blue and hot like vanilla ice cream
and the death of old leaves
sometimes death is beautiful
red and orange and gold
molding all your aspirations into a final statement
wishing on the scattering seeds of a dandelion
the glowing eyes of cancer victims
the ethereal limp
of the elderly feeding
on vegetable soup and leftover bread
so harshly compared to
the sick smell of hospitals
stale ammonia urine
crusted chocolate pudding stuck
to the corners of mouths

halls filled with vacant looking eyes
cows slaughtered and fat
fed on antibiotics and
chemically altered grains
the sick smell of stale sadness
the single thought process of an animal's raped life
~~still death is beautiful~~
sadness spewed out in stale tobacco breath
the putrid smell of cheap cigarettes
eyes which are red but never tear
dried up on coffee and routine
soothed by the bitter taste of coffee,
I looked at my grief
swirled up in the cream...

heaps of situation that you couldn't deal with stacked like
paperwork waiting to be sorted through i said it's all over but the
aftermath
still has me buzzing
like an electric battery sparking whenever
it gets too close to the rain
"fuck," i whisper to the non-existent air
I'm lost in my own
self-consciousness like a
bubble that no one can break though
am i a feminist?
how could i not be
my femaleness speaks to me
over coffee over tea
i said my body holds more
it holds more grief
each curve of my body tells a story
words written
not so abstractly
along the curve from my breasts to my hip bones
told in the twilight of my pain
words broken to the sleet and gray sky
isn't the whole world trying to tell you how i feel?
it's the space between our faces before we kiss
everything unsaid escapes my mouth in a sigh

and hits hard against your teeth
and it could never be true
what is truth?
nonsense encased in
fear and accelerated heart rates?
I drown myself again in the shower
my curls sticking to my neck and down my back
water cascades from my breasts
to my hips down my thighs
I'm buying time now
a constant need to purge thoughts from my mind
substances from my body
i said i have a leak
an inability to hold life.
have you ever stared up at the sky?
half covered in mist and stars and clouds
the cold exhale of your breath carries
words that mean nothing across an abyss
of which you have no hopes of crossing
you might as well
sing love poems to the silent moon
swooning at your own attempts at romance
clashing with the destruction
of tea that will never be drunk.

cinnamon rolls

trying to say something different but
it always comes back
to the same damn thing because i'm in the same damn place,
i'm trying to connect my heart to my words
and cut out the middleman (my brain)
trying trying, but the words pull themselves apart
like cinnamon rolls all partially digested,
knee deep into hamburger grief,
there's chocolate ice cream stuck to my arm
and you ask, "does heartburn make your wrist hurt?"
i laugh because i know what you're talking about,
i'm still watching that bleached out sun rise.......
is it embarrassing to talk about that grief?
that feeling the sunspot smoking hot feeling
of letting go?
It's like smoking expels the grief,
the hamburger grief.

fall away

fall away,
   i say.
fall away,
   for i fall into this love.
deep as infinite blue,
   red phosphorescents that tickle my heart
      in champagne bubbles.
fall away,
   i want no more but love.
this is not the beginning.
maybe i will speed from this now,
into twirling collective consciousness.
i sit empty and heavy,
leaving those known in love
as unknown.
showing my ego its ever present misfortune.
i lay waiting for you,
soft hand in mine on the mountain.
i wish for your kiss,
no defining it.
will i be welcome,
my long mane of mistakes,
tangled pride and lies?
i was a thief, a bum, a murderer.
i held hearts in cages of sweet words.
i clutched myself in love,
rubbing lust in mirrors.

no way to describe

no way to describe,
bamboo lash works framed by my mind,
tree trumpets of green spear clusters,
broken only by wind shifted blue sky backdrops.
this symmetry scattered in emerald chaos,
an army of living pick up sticks,
breathing silently, in long serene breaths.
such a host, as to include more guests
within its carnal house,
than the very space which it invades.
no stem leaning, that is not art,
but a vast web of clash and contrast,
smooth and subtle in its entirety,
itself only a fractal.

fall

the stars twist themselves in knots around me
knocking me to my knees
and i'm all sticky sweat
and hot from breathing,
the moon bright like skeletal teeth
making the ashen fields glow orange,
crickets and this cold air
feeling the beating earth
and stepping in these puddles.
the cold water on my feet
in a sweatshirt and flip flops, ratty hair
and still i remember that august night
when you fell in love with me
the pace of your lips moving to mine
the first time we kissed my world crumbled
so intense like shards of glass
which broke, and i bleed still
like the drops of blood i used to create on my wrist
dripping down into the marred scarred myriad of skin
of blue eyes that stared into yours
lost in this sea of possibility
and run toward the breaking sun
and i can't, i can't
it's the rumba
slow and sweet
i'm dancing silently
in my eyes we're swaying on the spot
and this boiled up pain is spilling over
until i'm cracked and leaky
spewing this red-hot diffusion
like so many pain-y salty tears
that burn my charred skin

Do not be envious

Do not be envious of others
for you have been given gifts
beyond your wildest dreams,
in truth things that God
have not dared to think,
but fleeting at the corners
of your bold strength,
and breaking into
this unique beauty.
humble yourself in
your ability, but abide
in your deep gratitude,
like roots search for water.
you speak as dark
as an Iowa sky,
and though you may feel
as small as the dark inside
of a seed in fall
your strength can,
can contain both you
and the whole cosmos.
Be humble in your
earth shattering beauty,
you may be smaller than
the kernel of a seed
but your strength
is as infinite as the cosmos,
as sacred as leaves
falling in autumn.

Let me be so patient—

Let me be so patient—
that my breath freezes—
my hope suspends in the air
and glitters like the last
low lights of a winter sunrise,
deep in myself,
let the word sing—
slowly rising like steam
off backs of lovers,
let my word break into
conscious thoughts
like waves shatter
their perfect form—
let my hope suspend itself
in breath so quiet
almost inaudibly,
you can feel my patience
pushing its resistance
to rise again.

When the time comes

When the time comes, I'll go
but no, I'm not ready yet,
life is fleeting but will have you
believing you'll be here forever,
moments in the sun can seem
like an eternity
never worrying about how
the story ends,
I'll wake up in the morning
and do it again.

Never knew I was scared of death
until it came to me
and my last breath was knocking
on the door,
too scared to answer the abyss,
thinking about all the things
that I'll miss,

Baby boys will never know how much
your smile holds my heart,
I could never let go,
I love you to the stars and moon and back
my greatest achievement by far,
how hard to think I could be gone from this,
vanished in the wind my arms empty.

My heart beats hard against the inside
of my chest
not wanting to fail me but needing a rest,
my lungs still filled with air,
purpose in my breath, I'm still here.

When I think of my life and each moment long
seemed like forever,
meeting in the park first kisses that never seemed
like they would end,

under the sky that stretched out
as i stayed in that moment

Stuck in bed unable to move from the dread,
contemplating how i would die,
could i survive?
It seemed unlikely and each moment that I took
seemed like a struggle of impossible weight,
laid some on me, too much to shake.
god forgive me if I can't do this anymore,
if I die now maybe he's so young
my memory won't hurt him,
is this the best way?

I feel like a burden, and everything i've ever thought
hurts me now,
actions that I never took sick like ambition
that I mistook and swallowed down,
how much time have I wasted?
this isn't what I wanted.

This test

This test, you tease me in difficulty.
i am lost in emotions twist, leaving it.
it snares me with jagged edges i have left.
i am torn, since born, of your divine dream.
i wished so much for stardom,
perhaps i cursed myself with it.
it brings me bindings and gnawings in my gut.
this self fights so hard to be
i'm drowning myself and it frightens me.
How could a poem be written

under my hand and never say your name?
it slides out in sheets of glimmer,
underneath my breath,
under my vanity and pride.
let it come, let it shower me in splendor.
wash me of my rusted self,
slow and heavy,
a ladle, i hang, suspended sip
above the ocean of you.
crack me, shatter me,
i desire your kiss,
not lips pressed on ego's glass pane,
not t.v. taunts, but flavor full.
why express, it has not been enough,
yet, is more to finally reach?
i speak, and speech in all its grasping
leaves me barren still, my will does sink.
why, why, why has my heart these aches?
set free the ego chain and wait
for love's tide to drown the bubbles free,
solid ocean, empty me.
this carousel has made me sick,
my maya's charm,
my magic stick,
my my, my me, me in part.
why don't you die and be just heart?

i said we're smart girls

i said we're smart girls
very aware of what we're doing
flinging ourselves at you
fling ourselves at the background noise trying to fade in
and i'll always, always be that girl
i hold it in my soul
i'm too slight my eyes are too big
my breasts are too small
for whatever reason
"My brain against my staggering pulse"
my sweet smile like like like
you know I'm going to give you what you want
it was never even even even
a question
because my life doesn't fit together
we joke about it sometimes
we joke about being outcasts because
because we never had that
wonder bread good looks
prom a normal life a
graduation ceremony
we never were that brown eyed beauty being picked up
at her from her doorstep
hairspray and bubble gum
pizza and ice cream,
normalcy runs through my numb fingers
i choke on it like a piece of steak
my sweetness runs deep
my quivering voice
my kind uncertainty telling you
that you can have it your way, and yet
our intelligence prevails,
we never were stupid girls

July 4th

my poetry lingers in my eyes,
lingers in my touch
like the moment that I revealed myself to myself.
I was lost in a flurry of voices
that silently questions myself
like a backspaced memory,
like I hardly knew.
I said my throat was like a damaged music box
which held the shape of words but not their content
my mouth hides words that I speak to myself
as I try and try to
stumble upon ears to listen to the hum
of my speaking quietly about the music of the sky
the endless black expanse that held it.
could I let someone into this colorless misinformation of beauty
which lingers in my peripheral vison
would no-one understand the meaning behind
my sigh like the back of their hand
I wanted you to know know know me, know me
like a song from a childhood nursery rhyme,
humming nursery rhymes,
sound box of words.

beat boxing sounds like the hum of traffic
and the coffee swirled dialects rich with meaning and presence,
love like blades of grass growing up though cement.
I can't make it sound any better, feel any better than this,
than the words swirled around me to some end
and I'll always be this little girl who contemplated herself
so hard in the bathroom mirror
couldn't tell if she was attractive.
couldn't seem to be complete like I would,
are make up till it cracked.
I can't seem to be

I can't seem to be
I can't seem to make sense,
so I wish at the sky
to take me into itself,
so I can dissolve in the atmosphere like a promise that
I could be different
it's like do I
think I don't deserve it?
do I wish I was different? Why?

I couldn't control it

I couldn't control it
when I was stalking through the mall
or smoking a cigar in my car
when I was in Victoria's Secret pushing my too small breasts
together
in a too small bra,
I could never understand how I couldn't see the outcome
but would still be unable to change, my body started tingling,
I can feel the grief in my body surmount my logic as I look down
into the cracked pavement by the trash can
and smoke one of Krista's Accents,
drugged up beautiful Kristy. with smile and blue eyes
"laugh now, cry later," Krist
she says what's wrong
there's chocolate ice cream sticking on my arm
and I'm trying to avoid, avoid saying anything
you see I bore myself, when I talk it's pointless.
I like acting without having to think,
I like the decisions I don't make, the kind I never even consider
maybe that's a bad thing
my compulsive and worrisome nature conflicts,
I'm a tame fire that's scorching.
I couldn't stand the taste of you,
sid and nancy tell the end
and I don't know what more I could say
love runs deep in my veins
I push people away
what could you see in me?
the mashed-up confusion,
worse than cold mashed potatoes.

Cry in my arms, little bird

Cry in my arms, little bird
Cry for all creation
Cry for those who don't understand
Cry for us, little bird
Cry for the future
Cry for the past
I'll let you go, my little bird,
If you will find the answer.

Where did all the people go?
Have you seen them leave?
Have they gone to paradise?
Tell me, my sweet bird,
Where did those who cry go?
It seems as though the people I knew
Have disappeared to where I know not.
So I will cry,
For those who have left and gone,
Cry for those who stayed,
Cry for those who seem to know.
Where did all the real people go?
The people who will cry?
Cry for me, my sweet little bird, cry.

It seems as though the people
You read about do not exist,
The people who are sensitive
and understand your twist.
The people who will ask
Even if they do not desire the answer.
Maybe they are hiding,
Maybe they are afraid to show,
Maybe it is because
No-one seems to know.
The only thing to do, I guess, is cry,
So cry with me, my sweet bird, cry.

I know not where you have flown
or where you have been?
Have you seen the people leave?
Do you know if I could go?
Over the hills I choose to fly.
Do not stop me, my little bird,
Just cry, cry in my arms, my little bird.

find me a home

find me a home for i'm houseless and lost,
tossed from your balcony for thinking
        there was an edge to you.
did i not love you like your heart,
was i not the drop of your wave,
        hold me in your crashes?
am i no longer longing for the
        sea spray's leap,
          no longer asleep?
wake me in your circling tide pool,
let me escape into your vastness,
let me be your feast and not your hunger.

I cannot hear your hell

I cannot hear your hell,
cannot let it rage at me
it's your sickly, sweet talk,
of the glassy eyes of bodies,
the way your womb shuttered lost
taking over your heart,
woman standing against the windowsill
discounted still till the end of this

like a waking dream I placed my heart in you never to believe
again
it stares at the corner of my being like the way the moon scolded
me,
the harsh light would scold me,
the hum of the earth beating against my pelvis, your voice
distinct
but fuzzy on the telephone

i cannot hear you yell
cannot let it rage in me
it's your sticky sweet talk
of the glassy eyed boys
the way your womb shuttered lost
taking over your heart
woman standing against the windowsill,
dissected
still
until the end of this.

I feel the deep emptiness

I feel the deep emptiness of myself,
yet it scares me less,
I feel the need to fill it up with less,
I don't feel the urge
to explain or justify it,
just the same empty arms
that hold nothing, gained nothing.

I am not made for this,
my ambition is misplaced in myself,
my ambition wonders
only within me,
what I want is too simple.

I feel this silence,
this lack of pleading,
this acceptance,
And I feel it all the way down
to my grave.
The cracks were never minded,
There was just a desperate clinging
to what was lost.

i guess i can't communicate

i guess i can't communicate, i guess i guess i'm all hate
i look down and cast all the brash judgements aside
and breathe into the center of my own fear,
i think of the unreality like my own private trip
my body shakes, i don't like it when you look at me
i don't like it when i feel like
damn man you're too damn close
& you're smiling too much
aware in every portion of my body that i am female
my femaleness screams
ooh no protect me
protect me
i can't talk
i'm scared every time my breasts move when i walk.

don't you understand? i'm crashing i can't DO this
i can't STAND for this i don't want you to come near i don't
want comfort i want to smash your head in again and again
against the wall till you're all bloody and small
i'm so SICK of it
don't you understand i'm not the problem just your unpleasant
reflection starring back at you from the smashed up fucking
mirror that you tried so desperately to hide but see, the pieces
always resurface from under the leaves, i'm all your tears and
your fears
i'm the fucking heartsick love song that you sing yourself to sleep
with in broken nightdreams while screaming
and ALL the broken promises you promised me glint in my eyes,
staring back into yours until you can't TAKE this until your
finest disguise will be a bunch of dusty old clothes on the ground
that don't even fit you anyhow, yeah that don't even fit you
anyhow...
i can poison you i'm not your muse i'm everything that you once
abused looking back at you with such an uncanny similarity TO
YOU
~come here, come here take this, no, no, i want to break this,
please break it for me~

break it into so many shards, pieces of matter you never bothered examining, just like you never bothered looking at me-i exist only as your assumptions ONE after the other crushing all the pieces together, all the pieces of me, until all you get is a blab of miscommunication, miscommunicating
yeah but you're the mis-communicator-
from your mouth leaks no substance, only words with definitions i can't PLACE
just out of place
yeah i guess i'm just so fucking out of place...

i have to write cold mountain trips

i have to write cold mountain trips
i lie on my back
the stars gaze back as if they knew all my secrets,
i pour my love to them, in liquid form,
which evaporates into the blue-ish black abstract of
everything that we are,
it glides with see-through wings
and tells me things that i dare not repeat
it rids me of all my emotion which comes tumbling out in a
fullness
that weighs upon my mind,
all this and my eyes absorb the sky
turning black and blue in their reflection
oh, all that as happened to me
i moan
i scream and sigh my pain to this night-sky
i shake and tremble at the indifference of the world
at my own limitations at communication
i state who i am to a passing breeze that will never
breathe a word of my true identity,
i'm on my stomach now
and the grass will remember exactly how my tears taste
i can fade into the earth
each feeling a separate piece
which pieces together the world for me,
i count my horror on the tree branches
and i come
tumbling back to who i am
suddenly constricted with these
hands torso face
my hair across my face.
flustered i breathe out,
exhale into the expansive space.
the stars wink back at me
i have now told then everything, they say
'dear child we are your witness,
we will never forget what you have told us,

come to me in your happiness and disfavor too,
our light will guide you back to this field and this grass,
even perhaps these tree branches which the moonlight bounces
off,
yes this same moonlight,
which plays with the shadows of your face
as if playing with a fun-mirror
and laughs with love, at your beautiful disfigurement.

I mourn the loss

I mourn the loss of who I was
Perfect, Madonna and child.
Think of this beauty
only taken away by my tired face,
the dark circles under my eyes
occurring because I was giving
everything to what we had created.
But it wasn't enough,
my sacrifice to our baby, to you.
It wasn't enough the sleepless nights,
and you fucked me like
you were somewhere else.
I mourned the loss of love
I thought you had for me.
It created a wound so deep
I thought I would always limp,
always carry my shoulders hunched,
understanding now people who did this.
Walking with an open wound is dangerous.
My tears could not persuade you,
my kindness was nothing.
And you smiled at me as you drove away
but it was only flesh on skeleton,
a reflex as cold as emptiness.
You piled body on top of body,
women all together,
and still I let you touch me. Again,
and it seemed rehearsed, you said
"you got away with motherhood
without a scar," but I hadn't.
You would not speak to me,
threatening my voice with your absence.
And still I stayed and wished different,
examined my perfectness in the mirror
looking for a flow.
That person died and even with
all her pain I miss her,
because I am someone different now.

My skin holds me together
and my softness is gone,
my voice does not waver as much,
but I don't have blind optimism, trust, health.
They say in dying you become
who you are and I have.
But that other woman,
she is gone by your making,
the other woman you didn't respect
and didn't listen to,
god, I miss her.

I wanted you in each breath

I wanted you in each breath
since I was five years old,
cupping the baby dolls
and bringing them close to my chest.
In wonderment I lost my innocence
that part of me that was carefree,
in each moment be,
impossible to change and then
I noticed that the past
was like concrete closing in
and each thing could never be undone,
so, I sat with my hands in my lap,
and I wanted you, like words never knew,
like I could never repeat
and each breath wanted you.
I was so confused, not knowing
I could just be used, but baby
you opened my eyes when I felt you stirring.
lives need to repeat,
and I could hear chapters being written
in your name, just a vehicle to repeat.
I was never very much,
my name will be forgotten,
but each breath went towards something,
you, and I can hear your chapters,
I can see through your eyes.

Because I could never do
what I was meant to,
my body was too weak,
I only had enough to have you,
so, though I may die,
I will not be gone,
you have my eyes,

I gave you what I could
which was never very much,

but it's all I had,
and I wanted since I was 5 years old,
cupping my baby doll to my chest.

I wonder

I wonder
If when you put your hands
inside my body
if you knew that I
blew dandelions out
with a wish,
to sweat to know
that life whispered on my cheek
like an invitation,
like the ground knew my name.

I wonder when you touched
the most sacred part of me
If you wondered what life
I had brought into the world,
the consciousness expanding...

I'm laying naked

I'm laying naked, the water falling from my sides,
       staring at the blue chipped paint......
laying there and thinking, gasping for air.
       I'm trying not to feel,
and it reminds me of when you used to hit me.
I am trying. I am trying not to feel the consciousness
       weighing down upon me.
    curled up in a ball, trying not to feel,
    and that's all I ever do, and it's a joke.
I imagine you seeing me laying there, my face red with pain,
   the gurgling screaming sound bouncing off the wall.
       tell me it's not real, say child,
   "this isn't earth but hell, and soon I'll wake"
       But you don't know.
  i know how i feel, like tomorrow doesn't matter
     and the sun only hurts my eyes.
And i hope you didn't hear that.......and I hope you didn't hear.
       I'm trying not to hear.

Me laying there screaming with awareness, trying not to cry
  while looking up at you hopelessly, panting and gasping.
And what you must think, my god, "Waif screaming in the tub."
     You tell me it's okay and that you've been there,
       and then you tell me how.
Excusing this pain, but you're choking up and your voice is
contorting.
    excuses laden in the air, and i wanted to explain my love to
you,
       how i wanted much to love the world.
But my throat is closing up. You look at me with desperation and
panic.
      While my gurgling pain bounces off the walls.
  The spilt water on the floor glistened, your voice is slipping,
    in your quaking voice you stutter stutter conviction less,
    you say "you're beautiful, you're a beautiful child of god,"
but the phlegm in your throat catches, and your body shakes
with pain,
     and now you're crying. And i know you didn't mean it.

you say "beautiful child" and your voice half scares me to death.

   You say beautiful child, it's worth it, but i wish i could tell you,

I want to tell you (down there sitting on the chair),
"all the love in the world can't make up for this."
your steel eyes focus in my direction and tell me
   while shutting your heart that life is worth it.

   Yes, shutting your heart so it won't spill over, so it won't break,

You say I've been there. Your pain makes me cry.
Hysterical girl, crying.....i want to whisper "i won't have your pain"

you're no longer a hurt six-year-old boy,
   and i am not the woman that hurt you.
   That is not an excuse and i won't comfort you.
Justifications thicken the air. Self-justified pity, and you stare.
   But i am not your burden. Nor your reason to collapse.
   But i am your mistake because i can't see straight,
      and everywhere i go people avoid my eyes...

love letter

woman- I stare into my own eyes
like a child weeping
I stare into my eyes as if trying to figure out my secrets
the ebb and flow of me,
I look at the curves of my body
my breasts
my inward slanting waistline and outward slanting hips
I feel the nourishment I provide
the gate to the unmanifested aching to be released

I am saddened by the loss of you
I bleed heavy
my womb weeps tears of a love I can only dream of
and that however brief
touched me with slight wings
and I love you so much, like this feeling I don't have words for
I will hold you in my heart forever
I hope that you can forgive me
my haste
my fear, my overwhelmed naivety
and that you will one day return to me
and I can outpour to you
my heart...

the treacherous gate
of where life breaks through
and breathes its sallow breath into the lilies of their hearts
the quiet acre of souls stretched out thin
their eyes closed, dreaming,
I breathed this small soul
sighing
and life
this dark soil
these swaying trees
the warm exhumed wind
this beating pain
I wished away.

I'm looking for a reason

I'm looking for a reason
Like sliding heavy stones onto hay,
the matted over hay
made with sweat and tears
and mud to hold things up,
But in the foundation runs deep splinters
extending down the base,
heavy marble could not have even held it.

The heartbreak was never repaired,
There was just a desperate clinging
to what was lost,
The way the last of the sun
clings to mountains
only to be enveloped
by the darkest blue,
unsustainable and beautiful.

It seems to move forward,
I must accept these cracks in myself,
these heavy wounds
barely held together, bleeding,
move forward with them
along the narrow path of life.
They no longer make me hysterical,
although they smart.

I feel the deep emptiness of myself,
yet it scares me less,
I feel the need to fill it up with less,
I don't feel the urge to explain or justify it,
just the same empty arms
that hold nothing, gained nothing.

I am not made for this,
my ambition is misplaced in myself,
my ambition wonders only within me,
what I want is too simple.

I feel this silence, this lack of pleading,
this acceptance,
And I will feel it all the way down to my grave.
The cracks were never mended,
There was just a desperate clinging
to what was lost.

I'm not here

I'm not here to pick up the pieces or apologize,
I'm not here to feel any need you have,
I'm not here to make amends,
I'm not here to be someone different,
I'm not here for you to vent on,
I am not here for you to desire.

I am here to let my softness be safe,
to find solace in the moon,
to tuck my baby in at night
and feel his soft fuzzy head,
to hold my emotions as my own.

I am not here for you
I haven't made it this far for you,
I am here to wake up in the morning
and feel peace.
I am here to feel gratitude
for my own life,
I am here to be at wonder.

I am not here to blame,
I am not here to gain my self-concept
from my own reflection
in another mirror.

In the light of day

In the light of day
you are a person blind
to your own angel wings,
But in the darkness of night
your dreams flow forth
With hope and love—
To find the morning,
you spread your wings
and fly away.

When you open your eyes
with the joy of morning,
you smile with the joy of day,
for your spirit remembers
the love and hope,
And in your mind, you see her
spread her wings and fly away.

Instant gratification...

Instant gratification...
I like things that have results
I like medicating people
I like the look of instant relief
That comes to their faces
A to B
IV push

But usually solutions are
empty promises,
and there is no right,
only wrong answers

Still, I try so hard to believe
in the heart of this Darkness,
in the quietness of the soul
that lives in all Things...
That relief can exist for us
Somewhere, in each other,
In broken bread,
Pieces of ourselves.

It's true

It's true—why am I
reacting like it's new?
Overpowering sadness
I reach my hand
Into my heart,
touching the sadness,
because I know
I already knew.

Why does the truth
bring me down?
I tense up and a
voice shouts,
Leave me alone!
"Okay, okay," I'm whispering,
because I don't understand
where the logic is placed.

In this place we, "the shadows,"
See how the tree goes from
green and brown to black shadowing.
It's clarifying then,
the sun is gone,
the blackness takes over,
I can breathe!

I love this darkness.
Something in my heart pulls—
my arms shake slightly
as I look into the truth
of the moon.
I can't see myself—
this is beautiful—
I can be nothing!—
but still I have
a sense of self.

I am separate from
the black trees, rocks,
sky surrounding me,
but that too is dissolving...

knocking me to my knees

knocking me to my knees
and i'm all sticky sweat
and hot from breathing,
the moon bright like skeletal teeth
making the ashen fields glow orange,
crickets and this cold air
feeling the beating earth
and stepping in these puddles.
the cold water on my feet
in a sweatshirt and flip flops, ratty hair
and still i remember that august night
when you fell in love with me
the pace of your lips moving to mine
the first time we kissed my world crumbled
so intense like shards of glass
which broke, and i bleed still
like the drops of blood i used to create on my wrist
dripping down into the marred scarred myriad of skin
of blue eyes that stared into yours
lost in this sea of possibility
and run toward the breaking sun
and i can't, i can't
it's the rumba
slow and sweet
i'm dancing silently
in my eyes we're swaying on the spot
and this boiled up pain is spilling over
until i'm cracked and leaky
spewing this red-hot diffusion
like so many pain-y salty tears
that burn my charred skin

La Résistance

La Résistance
Buying what they're selling I'm yelling
the harsh words break apart my lips, slip through my fingertips
and i'm looking at the ground
my heart beating hollow in my chest, I'm unrested
churning churning constant thinking
waiting for the moment of completion
of looking at the sky and feeling at peace
and the slow breath of life exits my lips
and my stomach relaxes, and this belly laugh escapes and the
quite quiet world will be open to me again

but is this harsh, harsh continuum
of built-up tension blocking my view?
it's okay these words are repeated in my brain
yet I don't believe them, there's always a problem
seeping under the calm of my eyes
bleeding out all of my energy and I'm so sick of it
I want to let this moment be in its glory and devastation
see the quiet complications and yet
smile at the cracked surfaces, the hunger the pain
the bad hair days,
the RESISTANCE
is churning churning trying to grind me away
you can't make it perfect
your pseudo control is worthless.

take the shady side out

take the shady side out
and disappear among the trees
where another life becomes
golden and pristine,
prick your finger
swallow me whole,
let's escape through
this pinpoint of light
let's get out of here,
your face is just
too sad for me
the corners of your lips
pull downward
and down down,
it's too cold to breathe,
it's to cold to breathe in here,
it's too cold to see,
intimacy escaped
out the window,
lost in the dew
evaporating still.
it's been a month again i know
it's been a year, and if i
wash away and
pull out the grey
and pull the fabric together
like good memories sad socker
like good memories blanched
and stretched out, forever
turning desperately to eat up
the grey which enfolds me,
and even if i had good memories
to last me till i was
a hundred and two
i'd still never fuckin' get over you.
And it hurts to some
unbearable degree

because every time i lie
i get slapped sideways
by and by,
day by day
my heart gets smaller
lifeless and tedious.
still the softness grows
one limb by limb
as truth unfolds.

Laundry Blues 2

you said you loved him because
he was the only one
who squinted through his eyelashes at noon,
to see if he could find rainbows in them
I listened to you
under dilapidated sunsets
the sun set blood red over half remembered spans of highway
i said i was just traveling though,
and this delight was more
than i could ever ask for,
it reminded me of when
in the back seat of the Nissan
driving though Spring Valley
I would breathe fog on the cool glass
and write my name backwards so the
Hasidic Jews could see,
later you told me
that they wouldn't talk to me
because my arms were bare
to pick up the sun spiraling down
over half eaten falafel
and wordless love.

"Finding your breath in my gasp" too gorgeous.
if I could write my devotion out in the quiet days that held me
the way one hangs laundry up to dry
in the blue spring breeze
if I could give you
all of my goodness
and none of my badness
you would have the remains of my love
which slightly ferments in the lines of my face,
which doesn't disappear
but hangs in the darkening sky.

Breathed to the cool morning
the expanding ache
of love which doesn't disappear but inhabits,

111

if I could take all the lonely glances at grass growing brown in the
sun
all the goosebumps of wind that was never expected
the guilty glances of middle school girls
the tentative hands
of shy boys
creeping around the nape of necks of girls
just to hold her
or the breathless quest of Monday morning,
of new sneakers
hitting the reflective black tile
or the expanding ache
of love that doesn't disappear
but inhabits the folds of laundry
like a quiet kiss,
if I could give this too
in my cold hands
I would cry stars
to the nightingale dark
sigh freely
to the glint of the shimmering snow
if I could take the moments of new breasts fitting into bras
and the sick swooning of crushing
and the endless procession of shirts
and the moonless madness
breathed heavy makeup covering shy mouths like a wish
I would sigh to the nightingale dark.

Let us decide

Let us decide where we be
If it's our identity
Or—is it just a mindless mistake
Purposely for the afterglow.

I told her my body was falling apart

I told her my body was falling apart
but she said to stay beautiful.
Like it was a choice.
Like beauty is more than skin deep,
more than the shape of your body,
it's something that radiates from you,
a presence that knows your worth,
your energy is beautiful, your touch.
She told me to stay beautiful
like it was a choice,
because it is.

let's go

pity is a useless word,
I have a death wish
the length of my hand,
that I hold close
to my heart
and never speak of.
Broken into fragments
like a language
I have no substitute for,
a hefty breath as
endless summer heat,
shallow and permanent,
like candy which
melts and slicks,
secrets like chasms of
dreams and forget-me-not
blur of actions that
lay thick and unable
to be altered.
I am close to myself
In my heartbeat,
i feel universes stir
and complete their orbit,
so quick that you could
only see a flicker
if you looked long enough
for it to burn you...

More than lonely

More than lonely,
i am here and also gone,
perhaps unnoticed,
the parade of senses tease me.
never left unsaid i say nothing.
pull me out of my shell, please.
pull I out,
pull I out, pull I, I.
let I be, as I should be,
Love and no necessity but Joy,
no broken toy,
no care but Caring,
no wrong but not to love,
Love, teach me Love
MAKE ME LOVE.
MAKE ME I.
LOVE I
I LOVE I.
I LOVE.

my child's eyes preserve the moon

my child's eyes preserve the moon
as distant
dreams weave throughout the stars
and are captured in his pen.
universes expanding
the reality beyond sight
and sense
did loom in such magnitude
behind your closed eyes,
pushing the uneven canvas
of your dreams,
bleeding from out your mouth
into the wishing,
stagnant breath of love.

not me

not me,
sometimes i forget,
or lie,
or just believe.
Yet i have written no poem,
sprouted no idea, nothing new.
i am the witness,
cut from the canvas by the painter's stroke,
painted of his fluid,
on his skin,
with the brush of his fingertips.
he laughs perhaps at one of his stories,
him in the sandbox, as you,
eating sand and grinning.
he rolls over in bed,
his bulging belly alive in mumbled dance,
clutching his swollen breast,
milk drips from his fingers.
he sits,
head cocked to the side,
tongue hung about,
waiting, for so much more than the bone,
perhaps, he waits for himself to see himself,
drop the bone,
and love.

ONE MORE YEAR

When you wake up each day
you're never the same,
These fractures in growth
may never be mended,
whether beautiful interstices
or having the feel and sadness
of jagged chasms.
And there will be a clinging
to what was lost,
before we knew better,
like the softest memory
of a light, before being
enveloped in the deepest blue,
this darkness.
Yet the heart remembers
the wet and cold ground
of spring, before we were
too busy being somewhere else,
the purest joy
always accompanying
the devastation of its loss.
Still, the embers remain,
and time can only do so much...
may you remain steadfast
in your wonder,
the origin of life,
this surrender,
the complete exhilaration
of the unknown.

RAPE

Listen to me-
Above the rattle of evening traffic
My voice-
Carries through the soft air
And touches your sunburnt skin
With vibration
The beat of my heart
Escapes through my throat
like a soft gurgle
and grows louder
my voice-
held in strained and compliant words
breaks free-
past the rhythm of days
which held me in their cocoon grip
my voice-
fragile like leftover leaves in winter
that are too delicate to touch and become dust,
my voice
abrasive like sandpaper
like cracked hips
and skin stretched over wailing bone
listen to me
sob up the split open words i couldn't speak
my voice
breaks free and runs like a brook in summer
listen to me
entwined in the sound of wind chimes
listen to me

listen to me
i have a story to tell,
my creativity which leeched out of my skin like a sickness
leaving me
coughing up words that i didn't speak
leaving me
shaking,
listen to me

in the soft night
summer dusk before the streetlamps turn on
listen to me
entwined in the sound of wind chimes
listen to me
like battleground bodies
like sobbing until you can't speak
listen to me
under cold sheets
the corner of the blanket becoming your best friend
listen to me
lonely mother counting down the hours of days
that held me prisoner, like the soft way
you brushed
the hair from my eyes, listen to me
as my voice becomes high pitched and hysterical
like cracked hip bones
and skin stretched over bone wailing
like woman child caught,
and i know your face
the paper white skin couldn't conceal you
all that makeup takes
the hole i hold, but it's not mine,
it's like food pushed to the corner of the plate
and i have you
to mean something and it took
all that my sexuality could offer.

Things in closets

Slanted sunlight
slid under doors
creating bordered silhouettes
of windowpanes on walls,
lizards with a twang,
shrewd and terminal.
Gloomy intellect pervades,
showing things in close proximity
their other half
with mocking parody.

Short Poems Undated

#1
Consult your resentment.
Speak up. Why?
Because silence is worse.
When you have something to say
silence is a lie.

#2
Take a drink of water
and wash your body,
the closest thing to god,
the furthest thing from sin.
take a deep breath
to replenish the life in you,
intricate design.

#3
Goddamn some people
take their suffering
and turn it into gold,
hold their pain so long
it starts to sparkle,
dimmed made coastal
contradiction.

#4
What was once light is now a loss
your fragile birth cursed me to no end
and now a darkness dwells in there
and bears no reason
for conquering.

#5
All the gold doesn't stay
but the pieces that remain
shiver brightly baby,
I didn't even know you
but you blew my mind,

how hard to capture a soul
down to the base,
I was naive to think I could.
does kindness count?
That space in your eyes
I felt I could fall into.

#6
lips curve is just a metaphor,
i am a fool for your gravity.

#7
This is nothing,
bring me wine
from its fine fermenting.

#8
Friend in Love
Sobriety.
No slips here,
Pure love and lost in amazement,

#9
Rain dripping and sightless air
        carries me there
   ...a reason to live for:
   none too bold to behold.

#10
So quiet that love whispers ahhh
Death so close that breath halts here and there
and life comes in heaves.
if only the separation of this.

Some things too perfect

Some things too perfect
for the mortal eye
are regarded,
Yet only she who dies
will see the other side,
A question don't ask me.

The song, the simple thing,
cast wearily upon
our mortal eyes,
I have seen
drifting through trees
in a someplace not noticed.

'Tis the song, once heard
through branches of
another universe.

See where it sings unnoted
It's the bird,
too beautiful yet for eyes,
seen by another universe,
its head nodding toward immortality.

'Tis only a question
not deserving an answer.

Stars were falling

Stars were falling as your eyes came out,
two dewdrops that outshine the night,
caught my running in a yarn of you,
tangled happy and spun out of blue.
      Catch my heart in your midnight stitch,
        you knit your love round me,
          supple mittens for my weathered hands,
          your fabric sails off free.
for i'm lost in your weaving dreams,
and i'll never find my way,
as your path is just my every step,
and your glowing lights my way.

We're only given so much

We're only given so much
to go so far,
she was always
her mother's daughter,
I was always
my father's son.
I reached into the abyss
of your absence,
trying to give love back,
but it doesn't look right.
the back of your head
left an imprint on my soul
when you walked away,
the shadow on the door
as it closed, not knowing
when I'd see you again?

I try to understand but
I don't know
how you could leave me,
I try hard to understand,
but I don't know
what's expected of me.

What is a man without a father?
does it have a word?
What is a man with a son
who still never had
his own father?
I'm trying to right wrongs
that aren't mine,
trying to fill gaps
but I don't know where
the puzzle pieces go,
trying to be a woman
when no one ever taught me
how to hold her heart.

I give everything I have
and I fear it's not good enough,
trying to build
without a foundation.
No one ever showed me how,
what's my life supposed
to look like,
god help me now.

Starve a man and he will beg for food

Starve a man and he will beg for food,
Induce pain and most will beg for mercy.
Humanity is weakness,
dignity can be stripped so easily
off your healthy shoulders,
the addict cries as if for food,
lies, steals, reduced to need,
a ball of want,
we are all so close to that edge
of primal need, dependent, clinging
to our illusion of control.
You had my heart,
this fragile beating thing,
this child, this innocent need,
a baby will die without love
and I housed one.

A child has no choice
but to love their providers,
naked and innocent in the world,
you held my heart,
this fragile beating thing,
I believed the words
that came out of your mouth,
I was not versed in deception.
But you are not my parent,
had no obligation to me,
my suffering was secondary to yours,
and we limped like that.
Me wanting love like water,
not willing to threaten our bond
I held each indiscretion down,
marked and numbered
for when I was stronger.
This deep well of ache,
these things that could
never be forgiven.

suicidal like a dot

suicidal like a dot
a car driving on a lonely highway
from the perspective of a drunk passenger on a plane
just waiting for the time to pass.
numb hands held tears
like washed over and acute feelings
that washed though me, like tears
and this is what i wanted you to know,
the beat of my heart the pulse of me
crazy artist abstract held in the light
held in the condensation,
the particles in the air hit by the sun.
"there's a certain slant of light on winter afternoons
the oppressed like the sound of cathedral tunes"
i'm tired of this old beast
how it worries hurts aches, seeks cheap thrills,
it won't listen to me, why does it hurt?
i want to toss this sick tired animal away,
it's not fair
being held down by mud and guts
and still the melody repeats itself
like a song you once knew
when everything was waiting to happen
how did it turn out like this?
my pretty but puffy face
hugging your leg like you were my mother
and i think i'm done
i think i'm done with it being fake
like this glorious sunset dying over the cold earth

Tell me what this is

Tell me what this is
I found you in bed
Eating dew drops from cut hair
Singing of heaven
As if you were there
One night I found you
Etched in pain
Unnamed
And ready for another beginning
Soft kisses upon skin
Sullen Light through
The burgundy curtains
When half the world was drugged into sleep
I met you in the air
The Shadows on the wall
Told you everything
Falling into eyes
You know it's possible
Watery caresses
I know you understand
When your mind's speaking, but you're not listening
i'm in some place I have not named
Between worlds
Where I don't exist
Humanity is a sorry excuse for a story.

when i dance

when i dance,
is not a generalization.
can a puppet dance the same steps?
I have no hold on my string tops.
when i swing them from the bottom i lack art.
I become a clumsy box dancing blueprint corners.
then i forget that i'm a show
and i let go of my strings.
and i'm swung free in liquid cradles,
set in steps i knew not and wouldn't
lost in hand and hand spinouettes,
with ethereal beings,
of alien form performance in one,
string jumbled chaotic love,
wonder pumbled, sway sunken,
i'm drunken on this other's love steps,
so glad to lose my mind,
on the wine of my lover's lips.

That

that which comes and completes
your lack of self stirring in the abstract
and this anger
the anger of this cuff I put on my self
out lash
do I have choice?
Do I have a choice?
The long echoed apologies and thank yous
I don't fit in this cliche statement that represents itself in my
mind
minding my business and slipping, slipping, slipping
into this girl
and there's no way there's no way to make it better
I lean away from you
and not because I don't like you
wanna make it right
tight
lost this thing.

the goodbye i know approaches.....

        say no,
and deny this heart its fear brushes
    and paints of paranoia.
your canvas is blank, without white
      and lacking black,
i find it swinging through silhouettes
    of borrowed color.
all these blinding flashes, bury you beneath,
    slashed in solitary moments,
      my mind comes passing by.
a carnival of color, trapped in the mirror room,
looking for itself, when it briefly flutters off.
"i can not find the spark," she says
      sitting center in the fire.
we turn corners of her over to find folds of riddles,
    the middle of which is nearer the edge
      than the in between.
i send whispers which mean nothing, to that,
    that which has told me many times over
      grow wings, it is not a metaphor,
      it is not a fable, story, fairytale,
      it is all those, and more so, reality.
      it is your body, when it is so close,
        that it is just an extension
          of my breath.

The process of un-doing

i want to sit here
in this closet,
as life passes me by
without meaning.
i want to sit here
in this enclosed space
for eternity,
with no fear,
no hope,
no memory.
--i willingly accept
numbness.
i want to lie here
as pictures form
in front of my eyes
telling me of misfortune,
And i want to experience
no empathy.

THIS DAY

To this day
Let me speak to you like a good friend
I've been waiting to meet,
Be thankful for all your hours and minutes,
Let me trust that each moment
That I experience, whether with great difficulty or ease
Brings me closer to this center
The sacredness of this time,
Of each second that has been given to me
I rest easy in the knowledge that he has held them for me
And will breathe in the absolute certainty
Of my required presence.

This hidden world

This hidden world,
to whom does it belong?
From the beginning of time
we have cast our confused thoughts
on the nothingness of darkness.
I see a shadow—it casts hope
of the one I want to meet here.
The cars disturb the silence—how rude!
She is alone, as I watch her
shadow in this nothing.
The beauty of cold
helps you design your thoughts.
"The beauty of cold," she whispers.

Nothing of importance,
nothing to be where.
Nothing of the far side.
This nothing of freedom:
It's just your breath,
like the smoke over the page.
The rain from the trees dripping,
The half-lit streets,
The woman walking home.
the smoky headlights of a car,
and then overall silence,
as the world lessens to silence.

How do shadows creating
images never seen before?
The only light is burning low,
then complete darkness,
like you never knew emotion.
All is enclosed in this
Secret of night.
How the trees look
when one can only see the bottom,
as the rest dissolves
into the freedom of dark.

The humming, sweet humming
brings you to sleep,
with a tear for the beauty of thought.
As you become nothing,
and nothing you,
You can only know yourself
separately from your awareness.
All senses are gone,
except one thought
in a space-filled universe
of black, splashing violence.
The water is black,
as the rain falls
in ripples,

this that is dying

this that is dying is really living,
this that is leaving is truly forgiving.
what has been fallen is more up above,
this fear and this hate are leaves of our love.

taste waves of slavery paving roads
            to slow us down,
ground channeling this band playing,
no real mixing but twists of tightness,
      might guess better things past,
            by last ways these days
      lay springs of markets madness,
   in cavernous hearts this carousel
            makes bright showers.
   these are tear drop magnets,
            burning love's lava,
            fallen bits of glory,
         watering these seeds,
      owned by their thick shells.

uhhum

for i am love
unaccompanied by sweet sorrow,
a fragment of my imagination
too trivial for your recollection.
all but one,
and one with everything?
i don't see.
for this can't be.
me.
laughing all over you.

We Break beats

We Break beats like beatbox magnets,
Madmen spin dwindling, kindling
Archaic language of Palm Sunday passages,
Messages blast witnesses, of this that is
all it is, always was so follow us,
ever growing glorious, flourish thus,
and catch the bus,
outrun the sinning lioness,
Mt. Zion is the final stop,
No stopping the eternal crop,
for Love's great growth keeps flying up.
the fear that keeps us crying cups of tears,
and years of buying slop,
the tops the toe of God and that,
is ever higher, flying past,
we'll never reach the very last,
and that is God's great gift to us,
we must ascend, towards the end,
the ever onward path of man.
Blessings on the journey friend
for we are one, at the very end.

We played games

We played games with the abstract
        of our minds,
not wondering to whom it may involve,
overwhelmed with cleverness—false knowledge,
into them we sought fury, and devotion to you,
        how I come here
  to pray for the beauty of words.

As you are nothing and nothing becomes you
    you only know yourself separately
       from your awareness,
      all senses are gone
       except one thought,
    in a space filled universe
   of black splashing violence
     the water is black,
    as the rain falls in ripples.

In crimson love explosion

In crimson
love explosion, this isn't a test
a conquest for some answer on the tip of your tongue
don't forget to remember
the kisses that life breeds
outside of me.
i promise to try
not to forget answers that hide right behind
            my insight
mobile life makes me stagnant,
replace myself with Styrofoam
skip to the center of love
and suck out the sweetness
replace, replace,
I want to mold into you
achoo, achoo,
skip to the center of folding bodies
and I am the center
my skeleton screams
without you, without me
asking questions of questions.
out-fold my mold
in greenery I see thee,
wet and green as in half-baked sunshine,
throughout trees
unseen in me,
i bide thee:
ask not of my mother the reason for birth:
i give birth to wings unfolding,
molding hopes of a thousand dreams in my quiet breath
i wish for a brighter tomorrow
of smoke in city parks
and a thousand things
calling you the sweetest thing,
calling you the sweetest thing,
the sun falling down and shining under hats and through glasses,

and melting the newspaper you're reading...
reading and drinking and thinking,
of the world falling, of colors that you've never seen.

You made me so happy

You made me so happy
when you were born,
Blessing.
Please let me tell you
You are nothing but
a gift to me,
That despite everything
I can only ever see you
that way.
Just as the rain feeds
the roots of the trees
You restored my heart.
The sweetest moments
in my life
Are mine because
you gave them to me,
thank you for being my child.

There's something

There's something
on the other side of death—
tell me—show me the truth—
and the truth will set you free

Heidi Schneider's Tattoos & Ashes

Heidi Schneider had two tattoos placed upon her body that offer insights into how she thought about herself, her life, and her work. The first is a poem by Emily Dickinson (No. 1005 circa 1865), which was imprinted vertically in individual blue cursive style letters along her entire left side sometime in her early 20s. Note: The lineation below differs from the standard printed version of the poem, enhancing its impact:

> Bind me—
> I still can sing—
>
> Banish—
> my mandolin
> Strikes true within—
>
> Slay—and my Soul shall rise
> Chanting to Paradise—
> Still thine.

The second tattoo, placed in black Gothic style characters on her inner left wrist, was the word, Truth. She had it placed there sometime in her middle to late 20s.

In accordance with her wishes, Heidi's ashes were scattered in the Atlantic Ocean off Myrtle Beach, South Carolina on 10 August 2021, in a family ceremony commemorating the 1-year anniversary of her death. This was a place where she had experienced much joy as a toddler, young girl, woman, and as a mother with young children.

Heidi Renée Schneider
March 24, 1986-August 10, 2020

ACKNOWLEDGEMENTS

Our heartfelt thanks to William Maxwell for inspiring the creation of this book and funding its publication, to Lisa Ewart for her hard work in preparing the text for publication, and to Heidi's dear friends Krista Feichtinger and Gabriella Wolman for generously providing Heidi's poems that were stored on their electronic devices. We are also grateful to Glenda and Alexander Schneider for their loving insights on Heidi's life and work, to Erin Pietrak for creating a compelling video memorializing Heidi's life, to Scott Amberg for selflessly attending Heidi in her final days, and to Lillian Schneider who generously covered the cost of special medical care and other expenses Heidi incurred in her final year of life. Blessings upon you all, and to the many nameless others who loved and supported Heidi, especially her fellow nurses at Columbia Memorial Hospital in Hudson, New York.

149

REFLECTIONS ON HEIDI, No. 1

I first met Heidi when we were both in our teens, at an alternative high school in Maryland. I immediately wanted to be friends with her, but she had this quiet way of being almost intimidating—she was so talented artistically, and on the quiet side, so you couldn't always tell what she was thinking or how she felt about something. We were always friendly, but it took a year or two for us to become close friends.

Heidi became that one friend that I could tell anything, without fear of harsh judgment or criticism—it didn't matter what it was or how bad it felt. She had this way of making you feel not merely accepted but knowing that you were truly embraced. She was also fierce, in a deadly, cutting way. Her quiet nature was not meant to be confused for a complacent, wilting willow nature. It was her way of taking in the universe, of breaking it down and seeing the different kernels of truth, ugliness, and beauty for what they were. It was her way of seeing the Truth of things that made her fierce.

Heidi was always an artist, with her words and with her ability to sketch or pick up a paintbrush. Her work showed her heart, and she was capable of speaking Truth from the Universe with her poetry. She was always a writer, a poet—until she drew closer to her passing. It was then, she said, that writing was too hard for her. Not physically hard, but painful, and toward the end the rawness of poetry became incredibly difficult, too heavy to bear.

Reading her poetry always feels like getting to open a door to something as personal as a secret and as vast as the open sky. Her legacy lives on in many ways—her beautiful children Nathaniel and Abraham, the love that we still have in our hearts for her and feel in our hearts *from* her. These poems are also her legacy, a collection curated from years upon years of writing, lovingly and carefully selected, edited, and put forth into the world to be shared.

I am eternally grateful for having known Heidi in this physical realm, and whether you knew her on this Earth or not, reading her poetry will give you a glimpse into a very pure kernel of her Soul and, I trust, feel a piece of that Eternal Love. Love you always and forever Heidi.

Gabriella Wolman

REFLECTIONS ON HEIDI, No. 2

Heidi and I grew up in the same house with the same parents but had such different experiences. Where I turned outward toward the physical-sense world and people, I think my sister often held the counter gesture. It seems to me Heidi's life, while grounded deeply in the world, held more of the inward, digestive, and creative process. Heidi took experiences and thrust them into her own being. Inside, Heidi poured those tangible worldly moments through her whole Self, filtering them through her own experience, distilling them into the essential Truth. Magically, Heidi was able to reconstitute Truth and create it anew through her own individual expression. Heidi had a deep connection with the sound, association, and meaning of words.
When words flowed out of her onto the page, they were complete, authentic, and held the world through her experience. Heidi's poetry holds her own words and more than her own words. The Truth speaks through Heidi.

Heidi and I are eight years apart in age, and during most of her life, a prominent theme is that when she was coming, I was going. It was not until the tragedy and gift of her illness, that we truly met in a space as free human beings. I am so grateful to her for enduring the physical pain to give us time together. I would be neglectful if I didn't also extend appreciation to my immediate family for what they afforded me to be with Heidi during her illness.

I miss Heidi terribly. From a relational perspective, she was able to listen, take in my experience, digest it, and bring it back to me in a new way. This is a process I personally strive toward. Heidi met me, and I believe met the world with Truth and the profound authenticity of her own inner life. Reflecting on Heidi, I see Beauty, I see Strength, I see Fire, and I see Truth. Thank you, Heidi for all that you give to me and give to the World.

Your loving brother, Alex